AQA

Chemistry for GCSE Combined Science: Trilogy

Foundation Workbook

Philippa Gardom Hulme
Editor: Lawrie Ryan

OXFORD
UNIVERSITY PRESS

Great Clarendon Street, Oxford, OX2 6DP, United Kingdom

Oxford University Press is a department of the University of Oxford.
It furthers the University's objective of excellence in research,
scholarship, and education by publishing worldwide. Oxford is a
registered trade mark of Oxford University Press in the UK and in
certain other countries

British Library Cataloguing in Publication Data
Data available

978 0 19 835935 7

10 9

Paper used in the production of this book is a natural, recyclable
product made from wood grown in sustainable forests.
The manufacturing process conforms to the environmental regulations
of the country of origin.

Printed and bound by CPI Group (UK) Ltd, Croydon, CR0 4YY

Cover: JOHN W. ALEXANDERS/SCIENCE PHOTO LIBRARY

All artwork by Q2A media

Contents

Any topics omitted from your workbook and from this contents page are Higher tier.

Introduction

Practice activities – Lots of varied questions, increasing in difficulty, to build your confidence and help you progress through the course

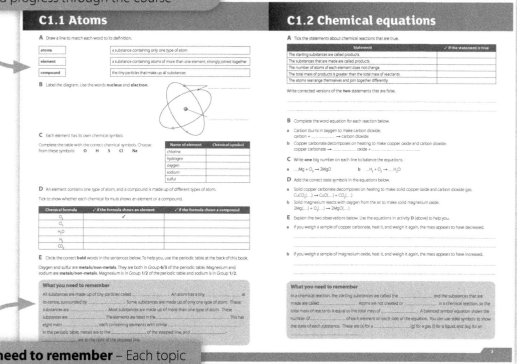

What you need to remember – Each topic from your GCSE Student Book is covered, and includes a summary of the key content you need to know

Hints – Handy hints to give you extra guidance on how to answer more complex questions

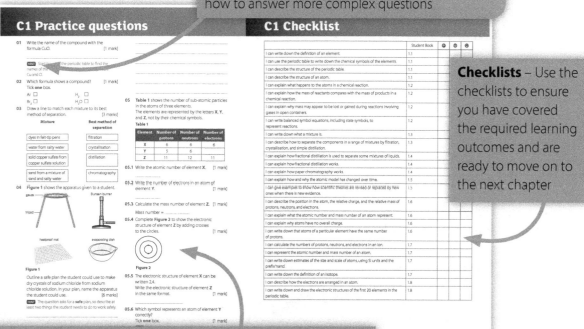

Checklists – Use the checklists to ensure you have covered the required learning outcomes and are ready to move on to the next chapter

Practice questions – Practice questions appear at the end of each chapter, to test your knowledge. They include a mix of short and long-answer question types, as well as practical-focused questions so you can practice the key skills required for your examinations. All answers are in the Workbook, allowing for instant feedback and self-assessment

C1.1 Atoms

A Draw a line to match each word to its definition.

atoms	a substance containing only one type of atom
element	a substance containing atoms of more than one element, strongly joined together
compound	the tiny particles that make up all substances

B Label the diagram. Use the words **nucleus** and **electron**.

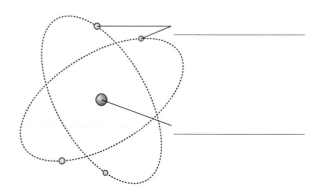

C Each element has its own chemical symbol.

Complete the table with the correct chemical symbols. Choose from these symbols: **O   H   S   Cl   Na**

Name of element	Chemical symbol
chlorine	
hydrogen	
oxygen	
sodium	
sulfur	

D An element contains one type of atom, and a compound is made up of different types of atom.

Tick to show whether each chemical formula shows an element or a compound.

Chemical formula	✓ if the formula shows an element	✓ if the formula shows a compound
O_2	✓	
Cl_2		
H_2O		
H_2		
CO_2		

E Circle the correct **bold** words in the sentences below. To help you, use the periodic table at the back of this book.

Oxygen and sulfur are **metals/non-metals**. They are both in Group **6/3** of the periodic table. Magnesium and sodium are **metals/non-metals**. Magnesium is in Group **1/2** of the periodic table and sodium is in Group **1/2**.

What you need to remember

All substances are made up of tiny particles called _____ . An atom has a tiny _____ at its centre, surrounded by _____ . Some substances are made up of only one type of atom. These substances are _____ . Most substances are made up of more than one type of atom. These substances are _____ . The elements are listed in the _____ . This has eight main _____ , each containing elements with similar _____ _____ . In the periodic table, metals are to the _____ of the stepped line, and _____-_____ are to the right of the stepped line.

C1.2 Chemical equations

A Tick the statements about chemical reactions that are true.

Statement	✓ if the statement is true
The starting substances are called products.	
The substances that are made are called products.	
The number of atoms of each element does not change.	
The total mass of products is greater than the total mass of reactants.	
The atoms rearrange themselves and join together differently.	

Write corrected versions of the **two** statements that are false.

_____

_____

B Complete the word equation for each reaction below.

a Carbon burns in oxygen to make carbon dioxide.
carbon + _____ → carbon dioxide

b Copper carbonate decomposes on heating to make copper oxide and carbon dioxide.
copper carbonate → _____ oxide + _____ _____

C Write **one** big number on each line to balance the equations.

a ___Mg + O_2 → 2MgO   **b** ___H_2 + O_2 → ___H_2O

D Add the correct state symbols in the equations below.

a Solid copper carbonate decomposes on heating to make solid copper oxide and carbon dioxide gas.
$CuCO_3$(___) → CuO(___) + CO_2(___)

b Solid magnesium reacts with oxygen from the air to make solid magnesium oxide.
2Mg(___) + O_2(___) → 2MgO(___)

E Explain the two observations below. Use the equations in activity **D** (above) to help you.

a If you weigh a sample of copper carbonate, heat it, and weigh it again, the mass appears to have decreased.

_____

_____

b If you weigh a sample of magnesium oxide, heat it, and weigh it again, the mass appears to have increased.

_____

_____

What you need to remember

In a chemical reaction, the starting substances are called the _____ and the substances that are made are called _____ . Atoms are not created or _____ in a chemical reaction, so the total mass of reactants is equal to the total mass of _____ . A balanced symbol equation shows the number of _____ of each element on each side of the equation. You can use state symbols to show the state of each substance. These are (s) for a _____ , (g) for a gas, (l) for a liquid, and (aq) for an _____ _____ .

C1.3 Separating mixtures

A Tick to show whether each statement below is true for mixtures, compounds, or both mixtures and compounds.

Statement	✓ if true for mixtures only	✓ if true for compounds only	✓ if true for both
Its elements can be separated only in chemical reactions.			
It contains more than one element.			
Its elements or compounds can be separated by physical means, such as filtration.			
There are chemical bonds between its different elements.			
The ratio of elements in it is always the same.			

B You can separate salt (sodium chloride) from its solution by crystallisation.

Write the letters of the steps below in the correct order to describe how to do this.

W Heat until crystals start to appear around the edge of the solution.

X Pour into a Petri dish.

Y Leave at room temperature for a few days.

Z Pour salt solution into an evaporating basin and place on top of a beaker of water.

C You can separate water from salt solution by distillation.

Label the diagram for the distillation of salt solution. Use these words and phrases:

water in   **water out**   **condenser**

pure water   **salt solution**   **steam**

thermometer   **beaker**

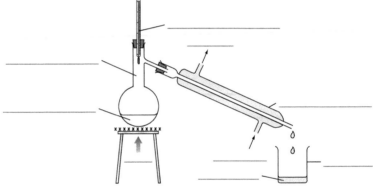

D Draw lines to make **four** correct sentences. Each sentence has one part from each column. You will need to use one box in the final column twice.

You can separate salt	from seawater	by distillation.
You can separate sand	from seawater	by crystallisation.
You can separate seaweed	from seawater	by filtration.
You can separate water	from seawater	

What you need to remember

A _____ is made of two or more substances that are not joined together _____ .

You can use _____ to separate a liquid from a solid that does not dissolve in it. You can use

_____ to separate a solute (for example salt) from its solution. You can use _____ to

separate a solvent (for example water) from a solution.

C1.4 Fractional distillation and paper chromatography

A You can use fractional distillation and paper chromatography to separate mixtures. Look at the chromatogram of different coloured dyes.

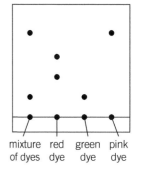

Tick **one** box to show which dyes are in the mixture.

W red, green, and pink ☐

X red and pink ☐

Y red and green ☐

Z green and pink ☐

mixture red green pink
of dyes dye dye dye

B Draw lines to make **two** correct sentences. Each sentence has one part from each column.

| Paper chromatography | separates mixtures of compounds dissolved in a solvent | with different boiling points. |

| Fractional distillation | separates mixtures of miscible liquids | because some compounds dissolve better in the solvent than others. |

C Write **C** next to the mixtures you can separate by chromatography, and **FD** next to the mixtures you can separate by fractional distillation.

a A mixture of water and ethanol. Water and ethanol mix together completely. ___

b A mixture of ink in a spot drawn by a felt tip pen. ___

c A mixture of water and liquid propanol. Propanol and water mix together completely. ___

D In the diagram, the thermometer shows a temperature of 80 °C. The boiling point of ethanol is 78 °C and the boiling point of water is 100 °C.
Write a number in each box on the diagram to show the correct label from the list below.

1 mixture of liquid water and liquid ethanol

2 This is the coolest part of the column.

3 This is the hottest part of the column.

4 Steam condenses in this part of the column.

5 pure liquid ethanol

6 Ethanol condenses here.

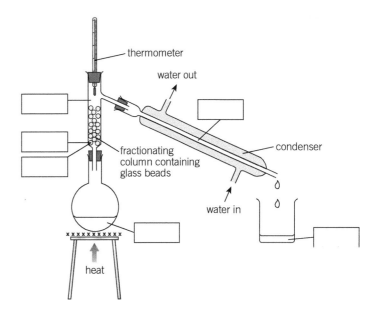

thermometer

water out

fractionating column containing glass beads

condenser

water in

heat

What you need to remember

Fractional distillation separates _____ liquids from each other. The liquids must have different _____ points. The apparatus includes a _____ column. Paper _____ separates mixtures of substances dissolved in a _____. The substances are separated because some of the substances _____ better than others in the solvent.

C1.5 History of the atom

A Draw a line to match each word to its definition.

proton	A tiny particle with no charge. It is found in the nucleus of an atom.
neutron	A tiny particle with a negative charge. It is found outside the nucleus of an atom.
electron	The small and dense central part of an atom.
nucleus	A tiny particle with a positive charge. It is found in the nucleus of an atom.

B Models of the atom have changed over time. The diagrams show two models of the atom. The diagrams are not labelled.

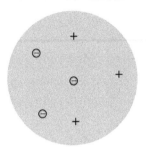

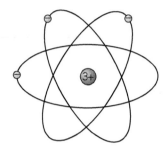

Thomson's 'plum pudding' model of the atom   **Rutherford's nuclear model of the atom**

Tick to show whether each statement is true for the 'plum pudding' model, Rutherford's nuclear model, or both models.

Statement	✓ if true for the 'plum pudding' model only	✓ if true for the nuclear model only	✓ if true for both models
This model includes electrons.			
In this model there is a dense positive charge at the centre of the atom.			
In this model the positive charge is spread all over the atom.			
In this model the positive and negative charges balance out.			

C A scattering experiment led to a new model.

Circle the correct **bold** words in the sentences below, which are about this experiment.

Scientists fired **positively/negatively** charged alpha particles at thin gold foil. They thought that the positive charge of a gold atom is spread out, so they expected that **all/none** of the alpha particles would go straight through the gold atoms. They were shocked when some alpha particles **went straight through/bounced back**. Rutherford explained this new **conclusion/evidence** by suggesting a new atomic model. In the model, all the **positive/ negative** charge of an atom is in its nucleus, with **negative/positive** electrons orbiting around it. The positive nucleus **attracts/repels** alpha particles.

> ### What you need to remember
>
> Ideas about atoms have _____ over time. Scientists gathered _____ from experiments on atoms. They developed new _____ of the atom to explain their observations. In the 'plum pudding' model, negative _____ are embedded in a cloud of _____ charge. After the scattering experiment, Rutherford suggested the _____ model. In this model, the _____ charge is in the nucleus of an atom.

C1.6 Structure of the atom

A Atoms have three types of sub-atomic particle.

Complete the table.

Sub-atomic particle	Relative charge	Relative mass
proton	+1	
neutron		
electron		$\dfrac{1}{2000}$

B Tick the equations that are always correct for a neutral atom.

Write corrected versions of the **two** equations above that are incorrect.

Equation	✓ if the equation is always correct
atomic number = number of protons	
number of protons = number of neutrons	
mass number = number of protons + number of neutrons	
number of neutrons = atomic number – mass number	

_____

_____

C The atomic number and mass number show information about an atom.

Write a number in each empty box to complete the table.

Element	Number of protons	Number of neutrons	Atomic number	Mass number
lithium	3	4		
beryllium	4	5		
fluorine	9	10		
neon	10	10		
gold	79	118		

D Circle the correct **bold** numbers in the sentences below.

The atomic number of phosphorus is 15 and its mass number is 31. This means it has **15/16/31** protons and **15/16/31** electrons. The atom has (31 – 15) = **15/16/31** neutrons.

The atomic number of aluminium is 13 and its mass number is 27. This means that it has **13/14/27** protons and **13/14/27** electrons. The number of neutrons in the atom is (**27/14** – 13) = **14/1**.

What you need to remember

Atoms are made of protons, _____, and electrons. A proton has a relative _____ of +1 and a relative mass of 1. A neutron has a relative _____ of 1 and no charge. An _____ has a relative charge of –1 and a tiny _____ . An atom has no charge overall because it has equal numbers of protons and _____ . The atomic number of an element is equal to the number of _____ in its atoms, and also the number of electrons. The mass number is equal to the number of protons added to the number of _____ . Atoms of the same element have the same number of _____ and _____ .

C1.7 Ions, atoms, and isotopes

A You can represent an oxygen atom like this: $^{16}_{8}O$. The top number is the mass number and the bottom number is the atomic number.

Complete the table for the atoms shown.

Element	Symbol	Mass number	Atomic number
carbon	$^{12}_{6}C$		
lithium	$^{7}_{3}Li$		
sulfur	$^{32}_{16}S$		

B Draw lines to make **two** correct sentences. Each sentence has one part from each column.

The radius of an atom is approximately	0.000 000 000 1 m, which is the same as	1×10^{-14} m, which is the same as	0.000 01 nanometres	or 0.1 nm.
The radius of a nucleus is approximately	0.000 000 000 000 01 m, which is the same as	1×10^{-10} m, which is the same as	0.1 nanometres	or 0.000 01 nm.

C An **ion** is a charged atom, or group of atoms. Complete the sentences below.

a A magnesium ion has 12 protons and 10 electrons.
So the charge on the ion is $(+12) + (-10) =$ _____. Its symbol is Mg^{2+}.

b A calcium ion has 20 protons and 18 electrons.
So the charge on the ion is $(+20) + ($___$) = +2$. Its symbol is Ca^{-+}.

c An oxide ion has 8 protons and 10 electrons.
So the charge on the ion is $($___$) + ($___$) = -2$. Its symbol is O^{2-}.

d A chloride ion has 17 protons and 18 electrons.
So the charge on the ion is $($___$) + (-18) =$ ___. Its symbol is Cl^{-}.

D Tick the statements about **isotopes** that are true.

Statement	✓ if true
Isotopes are atoms of the same element with different numbers of neutrons.	
Isotopes of an element have the same mass number but different atomic numbers.	
Samples of different isotopes of an element have different physical properties.	
Samples of different isotopes of an element have different chemical properties.	
The symbols show two isotopes of the same element: $^{14}_{6}C$ and $^{12}_{6}C$.	

Write corrected versions of the **two** statements that are false.

_____

_____

What you need to remember

You can represent an atom of an element using this notation: $^{7}_{3}Li$. The top number is the _____ number and the bottom number is the _____ number. A charged atom is called an _____. If an atom gains electrons it forms a _____ ion. If an atom loses electrons it forms a _____ ion. Atoms of the same element with different numbers of neutrons are called _____.

C1.8 Electronic structures

A In the model of the atom, the electrons orbit the nucleus.

Circle the correct **bold** words in the sentences below.

Electrons/protons are arranged around the nucleus in shells. Each shell represents a different **electron/energy** level. The shell nearest the nucleus shows the **highest/lowest** energy level. In an atom, the electrons fill up the **highest/lowest** energy level first.

B Each energy level can hold a maximum number of electrons before the next energy level starts to fill up.

Complete the second column of the table below.

Energy level	Maximum number of electrons in this energy level
1 (shown nearest the nucleus)	
2	
3	

C Write the **electronic structure** for each atom shown below. The first one has been done for you.

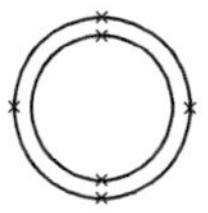

Electronic structure is 2,4.

b 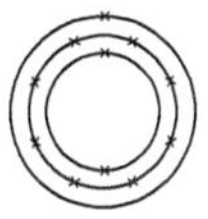 Electronic structure is _____ .

a 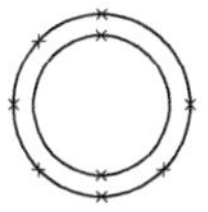 Electronic structure is _____ .

c 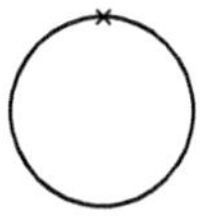 Electronic structure is _____ .

D Which list shows electronic structures of elements that are all in the same group of the periodic table?

Circle the correct letter.

P 2.8.1   2.8.2   2.8.3

Q 2   2.1   2.2

R 2.8.5   2.8.6   2.8.7

S 2.1   2.8.1   2.8.8.1

E Write the letters **NG** next to each statement below that is true for the **noble gases**.

a The noble gases are in Group 0 of the periodic table.

b The noble gases are unreactive.

c The atoms of noble gases have stable electron arrangements.

d The noble gases are very reactive.

e An atom of any noble gas has 8 electrons in its outer shell.

f A helium atom has 2 electrons in its outer shell.

What you need to remember

The electrons in an atom are arranged in _____ levels, or shells. The _____ energy level is nearest to the nucleus. This is the first shell and it can hold up to two _____ . The next energy level is the second shell which can hold up to _____ electrons. The chemical _____ of an element depend on the number of electrons in the _____ shell of its atoms.

01 Write the name of the compound with the formula CuO. [1 mark]

_____

> **HINT** Start by using the periodic table to find the names of the elements with the chemical symbols Cu and O.

02 Which formula shows a compound? [1 mark]
Tick **one** box.

Ar ☐ H_2 ☐

Br_2 ☐ H_2O ☐

03 Draw a line to match each mixture to its best method of separation. [3 marks]

Mixture	Best method of separation
dyes in felt-tip pens	filtration
water from salty water	crystallisation
solid copper sulfate from copper sulfate solution	distillation
sand from a mixture of sand and salty water	chromatography

04 **Figure 1** shows the apparatus given to a student.

Figure 1

Outline a safe plan the student could use to make dry crystals of sodium chloride from sodium chloride solution. In your plan, name the apparatus the student could use. [6 marks]

> **HINT** The question asks for a **safe** plan, so describe at least two things the student needs to do to work safely.

_____

_____

_____

_____

_____

_____

_____

_____

_____

_____

05 **Table 1** shows the number of sub-atomic particles in the atoms of three elements.
The elements are represented by the letters **X**, **Y**, and **Z**, not by their chemical symbols.

Table 1

Element	Number of protons	Number of neutrons	Number of electrons
X	6	6	6
Y	5	6	
Z	11	12	11

05.1 Write the atomic number of element **X**. [1 mark]

_____

05.2 Write the number of electrons in an atom of element **Y**. [1 mark]

_____

05.3 Calculate the mass number of element **Z**. [1 mark]

Mass number = _____

05.4 Complete **Figure 2** to show the electronic structure of element **Z** by adding crosses to the circles. [1 mark]

Figure 2

05.5 The electronic structure of element **X** can be written 2,4.
Write the electronic structure of element **Z** in the same format. [1 mark]

_____

05.6 Which symbol represents an atom of element **Y** correctly?
Tick **one** box. [1 mark]

> **HINT** The top number shows the mass number.

$^{11}_{5}Y$ ☐ $^{6}_{5}Y$ ☐

$^{11}_{6}Y$ ☐ $^{5}_{6}Y$ ☐

C1 Checklist

	Student Book	☺	😐	☹
I can write down the definition of an element.	1.1			
I can use the periodic table to write down the chemical symbols of the elements.	1.1			
I can describe the structure of the periodic table.	1.1			
I can describe the structure of an atom.	1.1			
I can explain what happens to the atoms in a chemical reaction.	1.2			
I can explain how the mass of reactants compares with the mass of products in a chemical reaction.	1.2			
I can explain why mass may appear to be lost or gained during reactions involving gases in open containers.	1.2			
I can write balanced symbol equations, including state symbols, to represent reactions.	1.2			
I can write down what a mixture is.	1.3			
I can describe how to separate the components in a range of mixtures by filtration, crystallisation, and simple distillation.	1.3			
I can explain how fractional distillation is used to separate some mixtures of liquids.	1.4			
I can explain how fractional distillation works.	1.4			
I can explain how paper chromatography works.	1.4			
I can explain how and why the atomic model has changed over time.	1.5			
I can give examples to show how scientific theories are revised or replaced by new ones when there is new evidence.	1.5			
I can describe the position in the atom, the relative charge, and the relative mass of protons, neutrons, and electrons.	1.6			
I can explain what the atomic number and mass number of an atom represent.	1.6			
I can explain why atoms have no overall charge.	1.6			
I can write down that atoms of a particular element have the same number of protons.	1.6			
I can calculate the numbers of protons, neutrons, and electrons in an ion.	1.7			
I can represent the atomic number and mass number of an atom.	1.7			
I can write down estimates of the size and scale of atoms, using SI units and the prefix 'nano'.	1.7			
I can write down the definition of an isotope.	1.7			
I can describe how the electrons are arranged in an atom.	1.8			
I can write down and draw the electronic structures of the first 20 elements in the periodic table.	1.8			

C2.1 Development of the periodic table

A Write down **six** correct sentences from the sentence starters and endings below.

Sentence starters	Sentence endings

The periodic table

Mendeleev

Because of isotopes,

classifies elements according to their properties.

some elements ended up in the 'wrong' groups when the elements were put in order of atomic weight.

changed the order of some elements to group them with other elements with similar properties.

groups together elements with similar properties.

left gaps for elements that he predicted did exist, but which had not yet been discovered.

lists all the elements in order of atomic number.

_____

_____

_____

_____

_____

_____

_____

_____

_____

B Choose words from the list to complete the sentences below.

> patterns   elements   discovered   atomic   order   gaps   properties

a Before the discovery of protons, neutrons, and electrons, scientists tried classifying elements by arranging them in order of their _____ weights.

b Early periodic tables were not complete because some _____ had not been discovered.

c In early periodic tables, some elements were in the wrong _____ if they were placed in strict order of atomic weight.

d Mendeleev left _____ for elements that he predicted did exist but that had not yet been discovered.

e Mendeleev also changed the order of some elements so that they were in groups with other elements with similar _____.

f Later, other scientists _____ the elements that Mendeleev predicted.

g The discovery of elements that Mendeleev predicted supported the idea that there are _____ in the properties of the elements.

What you need to remember

The periodic table lists all the _____, and arranges them in an order so that elements with similar _____ are grouped together. It is called the periodic table because of the regularly _____ patterns in the properties of the elements. Mendeleev left gaps for some _____.

When these elements were later discovered, the scientific community accepted Mendeleev's _____ table.

C2.2 Electronic structures and the periodic table

A Write each property below in the correct column of the table.

high melting point   **low melting point**   **brittle**

ductile (can be pulled into wires)   **malleable** (can be hammered into shapes)

Properties that are typical of metals	Properties that are typical of non-metals

B Tick the statements below that are true.

Statement	✓ if true
In the periodic table, the elements are arranged in order of decreasing atomic number from left to right across a period (horizontal row).	
In the periodic table, elements in the same group have the same number of electrons in their outer shell.	
Elements in the same group of the periodic table have similar chemical reactions.	
Metals react to form positive ions.	

Write a corrected version of the **one** statement above that is false.

_____

_____

C On the periodic table on the right:

- colour the Group 0 elements red
- colour the Group 2 elements blue
- colour the transition metals yellow
- colour all the non-metals grey.

D The table shows data for some elements in Group 0 of the periodic table, listed in order from the top down.

Element	Melting point in °C	Boiling point in °C
helium	−270	−269
neon	−249	−246
argon	−189	−186
krypton	−157	−152

Circle the correct **bold** words in the sentences below.

From top to bottom of the group, the melting point **increases/decreases**.

From top to bottom of the group, the boiling point **increases/decreases**.

The elements of Group 0 are in the **solid/liquid/gas** state at room temperature (20 °C).

What you need to remember

The _____ number of an element gives its position in the periodic table. For Groups 1, 2, 3, 4, 5, 6, and 7 the number of _____ in the outer shell is the same as the group number of the element, and determines its _____ properties. The noble gases in Group _____ are unreactive because their _____ structures are stable.

C2.3 Group 1 – the alkali metals

A Group 1 is on the left-hand side of the periodic table.

Circle the correct **bold** words in the sentences below.

The elements in Group 1 are called the **alkali/transition** metals. The elements have **dissimilar/similar** properties because their atoms have similar electronic structures. They all have one electron in the **inner/outer** shell. The elements are very **reactive/unreactive** because they need to lose only one electron to get the **unstable/stable** electronic structure of a noble gas. From top to bottom of the group, the elements get **more/less** reactive.

B The alkali metals react with oxygen, with water, and with chlorine.

Draw lines to make **five** correct sentences. Each sentence has one part from each column.

When you expose an alkali metal to air	it fizzes	because a layer of oxide forms.
When you burn an alkali metal in chlorine	it makes a white product,	because it is less dense than water.
When you place an alkali metal in water	its surface goes dull	which is a chloride.
When you place sodium in water	the solution becomes purple	because hydrogen gas forms.
When you place an alkali metal in water with universal indicator	it floats	because one of the products is alkaline.

C Complete the word equations.

lithium + _____ → lithium oxide

sodium + chlorine → _____ _____

potassium + water → potassium hydroxide + _____

sodium + water → _____ _____ + hydrogen

D Write **one** big number in each gap to balance the equations.

a ___ $Na + Cl_2 \rightarrow 2NaCl$

b $4Li + O_2 \rightarrow$ ___ Li_2O

c $2K + 2H_2O \rightarrow$ ___ $KOH + H_2$

d ___ $Li + Cl_2 \rightarrow$ ___ $LiCl$

e ___ $Na + O_2 \rightarrow$ ___ Na_2O

E Rubidium is near the bottom of Group 1.

a Predict what you would observe if some rubidium was placed in water mixed with a little universal indicator.

_____

_____

b Write a word equation for the reaction you predict.

_____ + _____ → _____ _____ + _____

What you need to remember

The Group 1 elements are called the _____ metals. Their atoms have similar _____ structures, with one _____ in the outermost shell. They react with _____ to make hydroxides and hydrogen. They react with oxygen to make _____. They react with _____ to make chlorides.

C2.4 Group 7 – the halogens

A Write a number next to each phrase below.

a the group number of the **halogens** _____

b the number of electrons in the outer shell of a halogen atom _____

c the number of electrons a halogen atom must gain to get the electronic structure of a noble gas _____

d the number of atoms in a halogen molecule _____

B Circle the diagram that represents an atom of a Group 7 element.

C Circle the correct **bold** words in the sentences below.

Going down Group 7, atomic mass **increases/decreases**. Going down Group 7, melting point **increases/decreases** and boiling point **increases/decreases**. Going down Group 7, the reactivity of the elements **increases/decreases**.

D Halogens form compounds with metal elements such as sodium, and with non-metal elements such as hydrogen.

Tick to show whether each statement is true for compounds of halogens with metals, or compounds of halogens with hydrogen.

Statement	✓ if true for compounds of halogens with metals	✓ if true for compounds of halogens with hydrogen
The elements share electrons in these compounds.		
These compounds include ions of halogens, with a single negative charge.		
These compounds are white solids.		

E A more reactive halogen displaces a less reactive halogen from solutions of its salts.

Complete the table below to show which pairs of substances react. The first one is done for you.

Pair of substances	Is there a reaction?	Word equation (for the pairs that react)
chlorine and potassium bromide solution	yes	chlorine + potassium bromide → potassium chloride + bromine
bromine and potassium chloride solution		
chlorine and sodium iodide solution		

What you need to remember

The halogens form ionic compounds with _____. In these compounds, their ions have a single _____ charge. The halogens form covalent compounds by _____ electrons with _____ such as hydrogen. A _____ reactive halogen displaces a _____ reactive halogen from solutions of its salts. Going down Group 7, boiling point and melting point _____, whereas reactivity _____.

C2.5 Explaining trends

The reactivity of the elements changes going down Group 1 and Group 7. Electronic structure can explain this.

A The arrows show how reactivity changes in Group 1 and Group 7.

Group 1 elements	
lithium	Li
sodium	Na
potassium	K
rubidium	Rb
caesium	Cs

elements get more reactive

Group 7 elements	
fluorine	F
chlorine	Cl
bromine	Br
iodine	I

Write the name of **one** element in each gap to complete the sentences below.

In Group 1, the most reactive element is _____ . One element that is less reactive than sodium is _____ .

In Group 7, the least reactive element is _____ . One element that is more reactive than chlorine is _____ .

B Tick to show whether each statement is true for Group 1 elements or Group 7 elements.

Statement	✓ if true for Group 1	✓ if true for Group 7
Each atom of an element in this group needs one extra electron to fill its outer shell.		
Each atom of an element in this group needs to give away an electron so that its outer shell is full.		
When an element in this group forms a compound with a metal, the atoms gain one extra electron.		
When an element in this group forms a compound with a non-metal, the atoms give away one electron.		

C Circle the correct **bold** words in the sentences below.
Use the diagrams to help you.

lithium atom

sodium atom

The outer electron is lost more easily from **sodium/lithium**. This is because the outer electron in sodium is **more/less** strongly attracted to the nucleus.

An extra electron is gained more easily by **fluorine/chlorine**. This is because an incoming electron is attracted **more/less** strongly by a fluorine nucleus.

What you need to remember

The Group 1 elements get _____ reactive from top to bottom, and the Group 7 elements get _____ reactive from top to bottom. When an element in Group 1 forms a compound with a non-metal, its atoms each give away _____ electron. When an element in Group 7 forms a compound with a metal, its atoms each gain _____ extra electron.

C2 Practice questions

01 **Figure 1** shows an outline of the periodic table. The chemical symbols of four elements are shown in the periodic table.

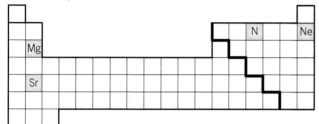

Figure 1

01.1 Write the chemical symbol of **one** non-metal shown in **Figure 1**. [1 mark]

_____

01.2 Write the chemical symbol of **one** element shown in **Figure 1** that is in Group 0. [1 mark]

_____

01.3 Write the chemical symbols of **two** elements shown in **Figure 1** that are in the same group as each other. [1 mark]

_____ and _____

01.4 Write the chemical symbol of **one** element shown in **Figure 1** that forms positive ions in its reactions. [1 mark]

_____

02 **Table 1** shows the electronic structures of four elements. The elements are represented by the letters **W, X, Y,** and **Z**, not by their chemical symbols.

Table 1

Element	Electronic structure
W	2,2
X	2,3
Y	2,8,2
Z	2,8,4

Which two elements are in the same group of the periodic table?

Tick **one** box. [1 mark]

W and **X** ☐   **X** and **Z** ☐

W and **Y** ☐   **Y** and **Z** ☐

HINT Look for two elements with the same number of electrons in the outer shell.

03 **Figure 2** shows the chemical symbols of the elements in Group 7 of the periodic table.

F	Cl	Br	I	At

Figure 2

03.1 The formula of fluorine gas is F_2. Explain what the formula shows. [2 marks]

_____

_____

03.2 Name **one** element that is less reactive than bromine. [1 mark]

_____

03.3 Chlorine solution reactions with sodium bromide solution to make sodium chloride solution and bromine solution.

Use the correct state symbols from the box to complete the chemical equation. [2 marks]

aq	g	l	s

$Cl_2(aq) + 2NaBr(aq) \rightarrow 2NaCl(....) + Br_2(......)$

chlorine + sodium bromide →
                    sodium chloride + bromine

03.4 What type of reaction is the reaction of chlorine solution with sodium bromide?

Tick **one** answer. [1 mark]

displacement ☐   electrolysis ☐

combustion ☐   crystallisation ☐

03.5 **Figure 3** shows the melting points of some Group 7 elements.

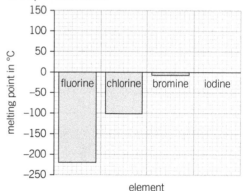

Figure 3

Describe the pattern shown on the bar chart. [2 marks]

_____

_____

HINT What does the y-axis show? Describe how values on the y-axis change going down the group from fluorine to bromine.

03.6 A student looks at **Figure 3**. He predicts that the melting point of iodine is −10 °C.

Do you think that the student's prediction is correct? Explain your decision. [1 mark]

_____

_____

HINT You must explain your decision to get the mark.

C2 Checklist

	Student Book	☺	☺	☹
I can describe how the periodic table was developed over time.	2.1			
I can explain how testing a prediction can support a new scientific idea, or show it to be wrong.	2.1			
I can explain how atomic structure is linked to the periodic table.	2.2			
I can explain how metals and non-metals differ, including their electronic structures and their positions in the periodic table.	2.2			
I can explain why the noble gases are unreactive.	2.2			
I can describe and explain the reactions of the Group 1 elements.	2.3			
I can describe and explain how the properties of the Group 1 elements change going down the group.	2.3			
I can describe and explain how the Group 7 elements behave.	2.4			
I can describe and explain how the properties of the Group 7 elements change going down the group.	2.4			
I can describe the trends in reactivity in Group 1 and Group 7.	2.5			

C3.1 States of matter

Solids, liquids, and gases are the three states of matter.

A Draw lines to make at least **eight** correct sentences. Each sentence has one part from each column.

| Solids |
| Liquids |
| Gases |

- have a fixed shape.
- can flow.
- cannot be compressed.
- can be compressed easily.
- have no fixed shape.
- have a fixed volume.

B Label the arrows to name the changes of state. Choose from the words below:

condense   melt   freeze   evaporate/boil   sublime

| solid | ⇌ | liquid | ⇌ | gas |

C Draw particle diagrams in the boxes below to represent a substance in its solid, liquid, and gas states.

solid   liquid   gas

D Energy is transferred when substances in the boxes below change state.

Tick the statements that are correct.

Statement	✓ if true
When ice is melting, energy is being transferred from the ice to the surroundings.	
When steam is condensing, energy is being transferred to the steam from the surroundings.	
When ice melts, its particles break away from their fixed positions and start moving around.	
When steam condenses, its particles become further apart.	

Write corrected versions of the **two** statements that are false.

_____

_____

What you need to remember

The three **states of matter** are solid, _____, and gas. When a substance is in the solid state, its _____ are closely packed. They _____ on the spot. In the _____ state, the particles are also close together. They can _____ over each other randomly. In the gas state, the particles are, on average, _____ apart. They move around _____ . In melting and boiling, energy is transferred _____ the surroundings to the substance. In condensing and freezing, energy is _____ from the substance to the _____

C3.2 Atoms into ions

A Reactions form compounds that may have ionic bonding or covalent bonding.

Draw lines to match each word or phrase to its definition.

ion	a diagram showing the outer shell electrons of the atoms or ions in a substance
covalent bonding	a charged particle made when an atom loses or gains one or more electrons
ionic bonding	the attraction between oppositely charged ions
dot and cross diagram	the attraction between atoms that share electrons.

B When substances react, their atoms change to get a stable arrangement of electrons.

Circle the correct **bold** words and phrases in the sentences below.

Sodium is a metal. Its electronic structure is 2,8,1 – it has **one electron/eight electrons** in its outer shell. In its chemical reaction with chlorine, each sodium atom **loses/keeps** its outer electron to form **a molecule/an ion**. The electronic structure of the sodium ion is 2,8. This is the same as the stable electronic structure of neon, which is a **halogen/noble gas**.

In the reaction of sodium with chlorine, each chlorine atom **loses/gains** an electron. **Chloride/chlorine** ions are formed. The electronic structure of a chloride ion is **2.8.8/2.8.7**. This is the same as the **stable/unstable** electronic structure of argon, which is a noble gas.

C Draw the electrons in the sodium ion and the chloride ion.

D Atoms form ions by gaining or losing electrons.

Complete the table to show the electronic structure of some ions.

Element	Electronic structure of atom	Formula of ion	Electronic structure of ion
sodium	2,8,1	Na^+	2,8
chlorine	2,8,7	Cl^-	
fluorine	2,7	F^-	
lithium	2,1	Li^+	
oxygen	2,6	O^{2-}	
magnesium	2,8,2	Mg^{2+}	

What you need to remember

Elements react together to form compounds by _____ or losing electrons, or by sharing electrons. When a Group 1 element reacts with a Group 7 element, each _____ of the Group 1 element loses one _____. The electron is given to an atom of the Group __ element. Both types of ion have the stable structure of a _____ gas.

C3.3 Ionic bonding

A Metals react with non-metals to form ionic compounds.

Draw lines to make **seven** correct sentences. Each sentence has one part from each column. You will need to use some sentence starters and some sentence endings more than once.

Atoms of metals form	between oppositely charged ions.
Atoms of non-metals form	ions with a single charge.
Atoms of Group 1 elements form	positive ions.
Atoms of Group 7 elements form	negative ions.
Ionic bonds form	

B You can use the group number of an element to predict the charge on its ions.

Complete the table below. Use the periodic table to find the group for each element.

Element	Group in periodic table	Charge on ion
sodium	1	1+
oxygen		
rubidium		
sulfur		
iodine		
magnesium		
calcium		

C Sodium and chlorine react together to form sodium chloride. The dot and cross diagram below represents the electron transfer during the formation of sodium chloride.

$$Na\cdot \;+\; {}^{\times}_{\times}\!Cl^{\times}_{\times} \;\longrightarrow\; \left[Na\right]^{+} \left[{}^{\times}_{\times}\!Cl^{\times}_{\times}\right]^{-}$$

(2,8,1)   (2,8,7)   (2,8,)   (2,8,8)

Complete the diagrams and labels below to show the electron transfer during the formation of other compounds.

a

$$Li\cdot \;+\; {}^{\times}_{\times}\!F^{\times}_{\times} \;\longrightarrow\; \left[Li\right]^{+} \left[\quad\right]^{-}$$

(2,1)   (2,7)   ⟶ ( ) ( )

b

$$Ca\!: \;+\; O^{\times}_{\times} \;\longrightarrow\; \left[Ca\right]^{2+} \left[O\right]^{2-}$$

(2,8,8,2)   (2,6) ⟶ ( ) ( )

c

$$Mg\!: \;+\; {}^{\times}_{\times}\!Cl^{\times}_{\times} \;\;{}^{\times}_{\times}\!Cl^{\times}_{\times} \;\longrightarrow\; \left[Mg\right]^{2+} \left[{}^{\times}_{\times}\!Cl^{\times}_{\times}\right]^{-} \left[Cl\right]^{-}$$

(2,8,2)   (2,8,7) ⟶ ( ) ( )
            (2,8,7)   ( )

What you need to remember

Ionic compounds are made up of _____ and negative ions. They are held together by strong electrostatic _____ of attraction. This is called _____ bonding. Group _____ elements form 1+ ions and Group 2 elements form _____ ions. Group _____ elements form 2− ions and Group 7 elements form _____ ions.

C3.4 Giant ionic structures

A The structures of ionic compounds explain their high melting points.

Circle the correct **bold** words in the sentences below.

An ionic compound is a **huge/tiny** structure of ions, called a giant ionic **molecule/lattice**. The lattice is held together by **strong/weak** electrostatic forces of attraction between oppositely charged **atoms/ions**. The forces act in **two/all** directions. This is called **ionic/covalent** bonding. A **high/low** temperature is needed to break up a giant ionic lattice.

B These diagrams represent the structure of sodium chloride.

Colour the sodium ions grey and the chloride ions green.

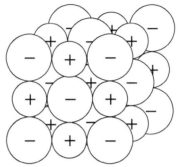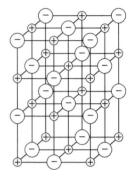

C Ionic compounds have distinctive properties.

Complete the table to explain some properties of ionic compounds.

Property	Explanation
high melting point	A large amount of energy is needed to break the many strong bonds.
high boiling point	
does not conduct electricity as a solid	The ions are not free to move and so charge cannot flow.
conducts electricity as a liquid (when melted)	
conducts electricity when dissolved in water	

D Ionic compounds conduct electricity when they are dissolved in water.

Label the diagram by writing the letters of the labels below in each box. You can write up to **three** letters in each box.

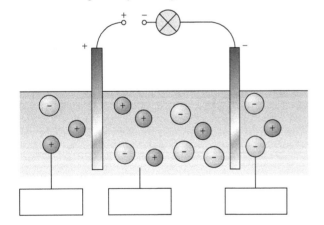

T sodium ion

U chloride ion

V Na⁺

W Cl⁻

X This ion moves towards the positive electrode.

Y This ion moves towards the negative electrode.

Z Sodium chloride solution. Only a few of the sodium and chloride ions are shown. The water molecules are not shown.

What you need to remember

An ionic compound is a giant structure of _____, held together by _____ forces of attraction. It takes a large amount of _____ to break these strong bonds, so ionic compounds have _____ melting points and high _____ points. Ionic compounds conduct electricity when melted or _____ in water because their _____ are free to move and charge can flow.

C3.5 Covalent bonding

A Covalent bonds are different from ionic bonds.

Tick the statements that are true.

Statement	✓ if true
Atoms of metal elements join together by sharing pairs of electrons.	
Atoms of non-metal elements may get the stable electronic structure of a noble gas by sharing electrons.	
A **covalent bond** is the bond between two atoms that share a pair of electrons.	
One shared pair of electrons is one covalent bond.	
Covalent bonds are weak.	

Write corrected versions of the **two** statements that are false.

_____

_____

B Circle the names of the substances below that contain covalent bonds. Use the periodic table to help you.

chlorine	potassium chloride	calcium oxide	gold
hydrogen	hydrogen bromide	nitrogen dioxide	sulfur

C There are different ways of representing covalent bonds.

Complete the table to show these.

Substance	Formula	Diagram showing outer shells	Dot and cross diagram of outer electrons	Diagram showing bonds	Are the bonds single, double, or triple?
hydrogen	H_2	H ⊗ H	**H:H**	H–H	
hydrogen chloride	HCl		**H:Cl**		
oxygen	O_2	O O		O=O	
nitrogen	N_2		**:N:N:**		triple
water	H_2O			O, H H	
ammonia	NH_3	H N H, H			

What you need to remember

Covalent bonds are formed when atoms of _____ share pairs of electrons with each other. Each shared pair of electrons is a _____ covalent bond.

C3.6 Structure of simple molecules

A Substances that are made up of simple molecules usually have the properties shown on the left below.

Draw a line to match each property to the best explanation of this property.

Property

low melting points

do not conduct electricity

low boiling points

usually exist as gases or liquids at room temperature

The forces between molecules (the **intermolecular forces**) are weak, so relatively little energy is needed to overcome them.

The molecules have no overall electrical charge.

B The statements below are about **polymers**.

Tick the statements that are true.

Statement	✓ if true
They are made from many small reactive molecules, joined together to form long chains.	
Poly(ethene) is made up from thousands of small ethene molecules, joined together in long chains.	
The intermolecular forces between polymer molecules are weaker than the intermolecular forces between smaller molecules.	
In general, polymers have lower melting and boiling points than substances made up of smaller molecules.	
Many polymers are in the gas state at room temperature.	

Write corrected versions of the **three** statements that are false.

_____

_____

_____

C You can use several different models to represent a methane molecule.

Give **one** advantage and **one** disadvantage of each type of model.

3D ball and stick model

displayed formula showing bonds

dot and cross diagram showing outer shell electrons

Advantage:	Advantage:	Advantage:
Disadvantage:	Disadvantage:	Disadvantage:

What you need to remember

The intermolecular forces between simple molecules are _____. Because of this, substances made up of simple molecules have relatively _____ melting and boiling points. Simple molecules have _____ overall charge, so substances made up of simple molecules do not conduct _____. Models help us to understand bonding, but each model has its _____

C3.7 Giant covalent structures

A Diamond and graphite are two forms of carbon. The diagrams below show small parts of the structures of diamond and graphite.

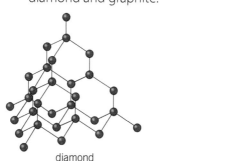

diamond

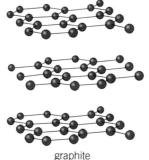

graphite

Some of the statements below are true for diamond only, some are true for graphite only, and some are true for both diamond and graphite.

Write the letters of the statements in the correct section of the diagram.

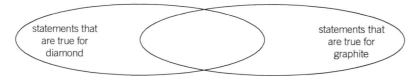

statements that are true for diamond

statements that are true for graphite

S It is made up of carbon atoms only.

T The atoms are held together in a huge network called a **giant covalent structure**.

U It is made up of layers that can slide over each other.

V Each atom is joined to four other atoms by strong covalent bonds.

W There are **delocalised electrons** between its layers.

X Each atom is joined to three other atoms by strong covalent bonds.

Y The atoms are joined together in a pattern of hexagons.

Z It is a good conductor of thermal energy.

B The column on the left shows some properties of graphite.

Draw a line to match each property to the best explanation of this property.

Property	Explanation
It has a high melting point.	There are electrons between its layers which are free to move. Since these particles are negatively charged, they drift away from the negative terminal of a battery.
It is insoluble in water.	Each atom is joined by strong covalent bonds to three other atoms. Large amounts of energy are needed to break all these bonds.
It is soft.	Its covalent bonds are very strong, so they do not break when it is placed in water.
It conducts electricity.	Its layers slide over each other.

What you need to remember

Some covalently bonded substances have _____ covalent structures. Examples include two forms of carbon, diamond and _____, and also a compound, silicon dioxide. Substances with giant covalent structures have very _____ melting and boiling points. _____ is hard because its covalent structure is very rigid. Graphite is _____ because its layers slide over each other easily. Diamond does not _____ electricity because it has no charged particles that are free to _____ . Graphite conducts electricity because the _____ electrons can move along its layers.

C3.8 Fullerenes and graphene

As well as forming diamond and graphite, carbon atoms can also form fullerenes and graphene.

A What is **graphene**? Tick the **one** correct answer.

K   a large molecule made up of hexagonal rings of carbon atoms, with a hollow shape ☐

L   a cylindrical tube made up of interlocking hexagonal rings of carbon atoms ☐

M   a form of carbon made up of many layers of carbon atoms ☐

N   a form of carbon made up of a single layer of interlocking hexagonal rings of carbon atoms ☐

B Which form of carbon does the diagram below represent? Tick the **one** correct answer.

O   graphene ☐

P   a nanotube ☐

Q   graphite ☐

R   buckminsterfullerene ☐

C How many carbon atoms make up the rings in a **fullerene** molecule? Tick the **one** correct answer.

S   usually 4, but some forms include rings with 5 or 7 carbon atoms ☐

T   usually 6, but some forms include rings with 5 or 7 carbon atoms ☐

U   usually 7, but some forms include rings with 4 or 5 carbon atoms ☐

V   usually 8, but some forms include rings with 5 or 6 carbon atoms ☐

D Why does graphene conduct electricity? Tick the **one** correct answer.

W   It is made up of positive and negative ions that are free to move. ☐

X   It is made up of positive and negative ions. ☐

Y   Its structure includes electrons. ☐

Z   It has electrons that are free to move. ☐

E Fullerenes and graphene have many potential uses.

Draw lines to match each use to an explanation of why the substance might be suitable for this use.

Use	Explanation
Carbon nanotubes reinforce composite materials in sports equipment.	Its structure is flexible with delocalised electrons.
Carbon nanotubes in electronic devices.	Drug molecules can fit inside the cage structure.
Various types of fullerene to deliver drugs to treat cancer.	Its structure has delocalised electrons.
Graphene to make flexible electronic displays.	It has a high tensile strength.

What you need to remember

Carbon can exist as graphite and diamond. It can also exist as _____, which can form cage-like structures and tubes based on rings of carbon atoms. Fullerenes can _____ composite materials, deliver _____ to specific places in the body, and be used in _____ devices. Another form of carbon is graphene, which exists as a _____ layer of carbon atoms.

C3.9 Bonding in metals

A Use the words and phrases below to label the diagrams.

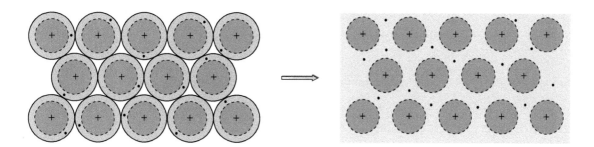

outer electron of metal atom   **metal ion**   **delocalised electrons**   **metal atom**

B Choose words from the list to complete the sentences below.

delocalised	crystals	electrostatic	giant
shells	positively	three	

a   The atoms in metals are closely packed together in a _____ structure.

b   In a metal, electrons from the outermost _____ of the atoms are delocalised.

c   In a metal, _____ forces between the positive ions and negative electrons hold the structure together.

d   In metallic bonding, _____ charged metal ions are arranged in a regular pattern.

e   Metals form _____ because the atoms in metals are arranged in a regular pattern.

f   An atom of aluminium has three electrons in its outermost shell, so there are _____ delocalised electrons for each metal ion.

g   An atom of magnesium has two electrons in its outermost shell, so there are two _____ electrons for each metal ion.

What you need to remember

The atoms in metals are closely packed together in a _____ structure. They are arranged in a regular _____ In a metal, _____ from the outer shell are delocalised. These electrons move between _____ charged metal ions. Strong _____ forces of attraction between the negatively charged _____ and the positively charged _____ ions hold the structure together.

C3.10 Giant metallic structures

A The properties of metals give them many uses. In the sentences below, highlight or underline the parts that show **descriptions of properties** in one colour. Use another colour for the parts that show **reasons for metals having these properties**.

a Metals have high melting and boiling points because they have strong metallic bonding.

b In pure metals the atoms are arranged in layers. This means they can be bent and shaped.

c There are delocalised electrons in a sheet of metal, so metals are good conductors of electricity.

d Metals are good conductors of thermal energy because their delocalised electrons can transfer this energy.

e Pure gold is soft because its layers of atoms can slide over each other.

B The statements below are about **alloys**.

Tick the statements that are true.

Statement	✓ if true
Most alloys are a mixture of metals.	
Most alloys are softer than the pure metals used to make them.	
In an alloy, the different sized atoms make it easier for the layers in the giant structure to slide over each other.	
Alloys include delocalised electrons.	
Alloys are poor conductors of electricity.	

Write corrected versions of the **three** statements that are false.

_____

_____

_____

_____

_____

What you need to remember

The atoms in metals are held together by strong metallic bonding to form _____ structures. Most metals have high _____ and boiling points. Pure metals can be bent and shaped because their atoms are arranged in _____ Pure metals are too _____ for many uses, so they are mixed with other metals to make _____ . Alloys are harder than pure metals because atoms of different _____ distort the regular layers. Metals are _____ conductors of electricity because their _____ electrons carry charge through the metal. Delocalised electrons also transfer _____ energy.

C3 Practice questions

01 What type of bonds join the atoms together in a polymer molecule?

Tick **one** box. [1 mark]

metallic ☐   covalent ☐

ionic ☐   intermolecular ☐

HINT Read the question carefully – it is asking about the bonds that hold atoms together in a molecule.

02 **Figures 1** and **2** show two models of a methane molecule.

Figure 1   **Figure 2**

02.1 Write the molecular formula of methane. [1 mark]

02.2 Write down what each line in **Figure 1** represents.

[1 mark]

02.3 Explain **one advantage** and **one disadvantage** of the model in **Figure 1** compared with the model in **Figure 2**. [2 marks]

HINT Which model shows how the bonds are formed? Which model shows the angles between the bonds?

03 **Table 1** gives some properties of four substances. The substances are represented by the letters **W**, **X**, **Y**, and **Z**, not by their chemical symbols.

Table 1

Substance	Melting point in °C	Boiling point in °C	Does it conduct electricity as a solid?	Does it conduct electricity when melted?
W	1063	2970	yes	yes
X	2852	3600	no	yes
Y	−78	−33	no	no
Z	1600	2230	no	no

03.1 Give the letter of **one** substance in the table that consists of small molecules. [1 mark]

HINT Can you remember whether substances made up of small molecules have high or low melting and boiling points?

03.2 Give the letter of **one** substance in the table that could be gold. Explain your decision. [2 marks]

Letter: _____

03.3 Give the letter of **one** substance in the table that has a giant covalent structure. [1 mark]

_____

03.4 Suggest names of **one element** and **one compound** that could be represented by the letter **Z** in the table. [2 marks]

Element: _____

Compound: _____

HINT Your answer to **04.3** will help you here.

03.5 Suggest **one** property of substance **X** that is not given in the table. Explain your answer. [2 marks]

04.1 **Figure 3** shows the electronic structures of a sodium atom and a chlorine atom.

Figure 3

Describe how sodium atoms and chlorine atoms form sodium chloride. Give the formulae of the ions formed. [4 marks]

HINT There are four marks for this question, so you need to make at least four points in your answer.

04.2 Sodium chloride has a high melting point. Explain why. [2 marks]

04.3 Melted sodium chloride conducts electricity. Explain why. [2 marks]

C3 Checklist

	Student Book	☺	😐	☹
I can explain how the melting point and boiling point of a substance depend on what its particles are like, and on the forces between the particles.	3.1			
I can write down that atoms themselves do not have the bulk properties of materials.	3.1			
I can predict the states of substances at different temperatures, given appropriate data.	3.1			
I can write down what a chemical element is.	3.2			
I can describe how elements form compounds.	3.2			
I can explain how atoms form positive and negative ions.	3.2			
I can explain how the elements in Group 1 bond with the elements in Group 7.	3.2			
I can explain how ionic compounds are held together.	3.3			
I can write down which elements, as well as those in Groups 1 and 7, form ions.	3.3			
I can explain how the charges on ions are related to group numbers in the periodic table.	3.3			
I can explain why ionic compounds have high melting points.	3.4			
I can explain why ionic compounds conduct electricity when they are molten or dissolved in water.	3.4			
I can explain how covalent bonds are formed.	3.5			
I can describe how to represent covalent bonds.				
I can write down the types of substance that contain covalent bonds.	3.5			
I can describe the limitations of using models such as dot and cross, ball and stick, 2D diagrams, and 3D diagrams to represent molecules or giant structures.	3.6			
I can explain why substances made of simple molecules have low melting points and boiling points.	3.6			
I can explain why substances with simple molecules do not conduct electricity.	3.6			
I can describe the general properties of substances that have giant covalent structures.	3.7			
I can explain why diamond is hard and graphite is slippery.	3.7			
I can explain why graphite can conduct electricity and thermal energy.	3.7			
I can describe the structures of the fullerenes and graphene.	3.8			
I can recognise fullerenes and graphene from diagrams.	3.8			
I can write down some uses of fullerenes.	3.8			
I can describe how the atoms in metals are arranged.	3.9			
I can explain how the atoms in metals are bonded to each other.	3.9			
I can explain why metals can be bent and shaped without breaking.	3.10			
I can explain why alloys are harder than pure metals.	3.10			
I can explain how metals conduct electricity and thermal energy.	3.10			

C4.1 Relative masses and moles

A Draw lines to match each term to its symbol and definition.

Term	Symbol	Definition
relative atomic mass	none	the total of the relative atomic masses of each element in a substance, added up in the ratio shown in the chemical formula
isotopes	A_r	atoms of an element that have the same number of protons but a different number of neutrons
relative formula mass	M_r	the average mass of the atoms of an element compared with carbon-12

B Circle the correct **bold** numbers in the sentences below.

Chlorine has two isotopes. In a sample of chlorine, the abundance of ^{35}Cl is 75% and the abundance of ^{37}Cl is 25%. This means that, if you have 100 chlorine atoms, **25/75** of them have a mass number of 35 and **25/75** of them have a mass number of 37. You can calculate the relative atomic mass by finding the mean mass of these 100 atoms:

$$A_r \text{ of chlorine} = \frac{(75 \times 35) + (25 \times 37)}{100} = \textbf{35.5/36.5}$$

C Calculate the relative atomic masses of the elements below.

a lithium, which exists as 8% ^6Li and 92% ^7Li

_____

b neon, which exists as 91% ^{20}Ne and 9% ^{22}Ne

_____

c bromine, which exists as 51% ^{79}Br and 49% ^{81}Br

_____

D Calculate the relative formula mass for each substance below.

a chlorine, Cl_2 (A_r value: Cl = 35.5)

_____

b magnesium oxide, MgO (A_r values: Mg = 12, O = 16)

_____

c water, H_2O (A_r values: H = 1, O = 16)

_____

d carbon dioxide, CO_2 (A_r values: C = 12, O = 16)

_____

e aluminium oxide, Al_2O_3 (A_r values: Al = 27, O = 16)

_____

f copper sulfate, $CuSO_4$ (A_r values: Cu = 63.5, S = 32, O = 16)

_____

g nitric acid, HNO_3 (A_r values: H = 1, N = 14, O = 16)

_____

What you need to remember

The relative _____ mass of an element is the average mass of the atoms of the element compared with _____ -12. You can calculate the relative atomic mass of an element by finding the _____ relative mass of 100 of its _____ . The relative formula mass of a substance is the _____ of the relative atomic masses, added up in the ratio shown in the chemical _____ .

C4.4 Expressing concentrations

A Draw a line to match each word or phrase to its definition.

concentration	how much space a solution takes up
volume of solution	in a solution, the substance that is dissolved in the solvent
solvent	the amount of solute dissolved in a given volume of solution
solute	a mixture of substances, in which a solute is dissolved in a solvent
solution	in a solution, the liquid that a substance is dissolved in

B It is important to give units for concentration values.

Complete the table.

Quantity	Units
amount of solute	
	dm^3 or cm^3
	g/dm^3 or g/cm^3

C Rearrange the equation below so that the amount of solute is the subject of the equation.

$$\text{concentration in } g/dm^3 = \frac{\text{amount of solute in g}}{\text{volume of solution in } dm^3}$$

amount of solute in g = _____ × _____

D Calculate the concentrations of the solutions below.
Show any working, and include the correct units.

a 40 g of sodium hydroxide dissolved in 1 dm^3 of solution.

_____

b 98 g of sulfuric acid dissolved in 1000 cm^3 of solution.

_____

c 4 g of copper sulfate dissolved in 250 cm^3 of solution.

_____

E Calculate the mass of solute in each of the following solutions.

a 1 dm^3 of a solution of potassium chloride of concentration 50 g/dm^3.

_____

b 0.5 dm^3 of a solution of nitric acid of concentration 63 g/dm^3.

_____

What you need to remember

You can use the equation below to calculate the concentration of a solution:

$$\text{concentration in } g/dm^3 = \frac{\text{amount of solute in g}}{}$$

You can change the subject of the equation to calculate the amount of solute:

amount of solute in g = _____ × volume of solution in dm^3

C4 Practice questions

01 How many elements are in the formula H_3PO_4?
Tick **one** box. [1 mark]

3 ☐

5 ☐

7 ☐

8 ☐

HINT Count the number of different chemical symbols in the formula.

02 How many atoms are in the formula HNO_3?
Tick **one** box. [1 mark]

3 ☐

5 ☐

7 ☐

9 ☐

03 Calculate the concentration of a solution that has 90 g of potassium chloride dissolved in 2 dm^3 of solution. [2 marks]

Concentration = _____ g/dm^3

HINT Start by writing out the equation you will need.

04 Calculate the mass of dissolved silver nitrate in 0.5 dm^3 of a solution with a concentration of 6.0 g/dm^3. [2 marks]

Mass = _____ g

HINT Start by rearranging the equation you used in question 3, so that mass is the subject of the equation.

05 This question is about copper carbonate.

05.1 The formula of copper carbonate is $CuCO_3$.
Calculate the relative formula mass of copper carbonate. [2 marks]
Use these relative atomic masses in your calculation: Cu = 63.5   C = 12   O = 16

Relative formula mass = _____

05.2 A student plans to heat some copper carbonate.
He weighs a tin lid.
Then he places some copper carbonate on the tin lid. He weighs the tin lid and its contents.

Use the student's data in **Table 1** to calculate the mass of copper carbonate on the tin lid. [2 marks]

Table 1

What I weighed	Massing
empty tin lid	15.0
tin lid and copper carbonate	27.4

Mass of copper carbonate = _____ g

05.3 The student heats the copper carbonate. He uses the apparatus in Figure 1.

Figure 1

Write down **two** safety precautions the student should take when heating. [2 marks]

1 _____

2 _____

05.4 On heating, copper carbonate decomposes to make copper oxide and carbon dioxide.
Complete the word equation for the reaction. [1 mark]

copper carbonate → _____

+ _____

05.5 Look at your answer to **05.2**.
Write down the total mass of products the student can expect to make. [1 mark]

_____ g

05.6 After heating, the student found that the mass of product on his tin lid was 5.6 g.
Explain why the mass of product on the tin lid is not the same as the total mass of products the student can expect to make. [2 marks]
Use the equation below to help you.
$CuCO_3(s) \rightarrow CuO(s) + CO_2(g)$

HINT Look at the state symbols in the equation.

_____

_____

_____

_____

C4 Checklist

	Student Book	☺	☺	☹
I can write down the meaning of the term relative atomic mass.	4.1			
I can calculate the relative atomic mass of an element.	4.1			
I can calculate the relative formula mass of a compound.	4.1			
I can write down the units for the concentration of a solution.	4.4			
I can calculate the concentration of a solution.	4.4			
I can calculate the mass of solute in a certain volume of solution of known concentration.	4.4			

C5.1 The reactivity series

A Draw a line to match each word or term to its definition.

ore		adding oxygen to a substance such as a metal
oxidising		removing oxygen from a substance such as a metal oxide
reducing		a rock that contains a metal that can be extracted from the rock economically
reactivity series		a list of metals in order of their reactivity, with the most reactive at the top

B Write each phrase below in the correct box in the table.

explode   **very slow reaction**   **no reaction**   **fizz, giving off hydrogen and**

forming a salt   **react slowly with steam**

Order of reactivity	Reaction with water	Reaction with dilute acid
potassium	fizz, giving off hydrogen gas and forming an alkaline solution	
sodium		
calcium		
magnesium		
zinc		
iron		
tin		react slowly when warmed, forming hydrogen gas and a salt
lead		
copper	no reaction, even with steam	
silver		
gold		

C Write word equations and balanced symbol equations, including state symbols, for these reactions.

a magnesium (Mg) reacting with sulfuric acid (H_2SO_4) to form magnesium sulfate solution ($MgSO_4$) and hydrogen (H_2).

_____ + _____ → _____ + _____

_____ + _____ → _____ + _____

b potassium (K) reacting with water (H_2O) to form potassium hydroxide solution (KOH) and hydrogen (H_2)

_____ + _____ → _____ + _____

_____ + _____ → _____ + _____

What you need to remember

The reactivity series lists the metals in order of their _____, with the _____ reactive metals at the top. Metals at the top react _____ with water and acids, and metals at the _____ do not react with water or _____ .

C5.2 Displacement reactions

A What is a **displacement reaction**? Tick the best definition.

W a reaction in which a more reactive metal displaces a less reactive metal from a solution of one of its salts ☐

X a reaction in which a less reactive metal displaces a more reactive metal from a solution of one of its salts ☐

Y a reaction in which a more reactive metal displaces a less reactive metal from a solution of its chloride ☐

Z a reaction in which a less reactive metal displaces a more reactive metal from a solution of its chloride ☐

B The reactivity series on the right includes **two** non-metals. Write their names below.

_____ and _____

C The reactivity series helps you predict whether substances will react.

Tick the boxes under the pairs of substances that will react.

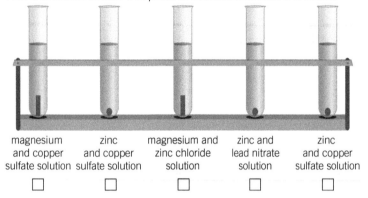

magnesium and copper sulfate solution	zinc and copper sulfate solution	magnesium and zinc chloride solution	zinc and lead nitrate solution	zinc and copper sulfate solution
☐	☐	☐	☐	☐

> **The reactivity series**
>
> potassium
> sodium
> calcium
> magnesium
> aluminium
> carbon
> zinc
> iron
> tin
> lead
> hydrogen
> copper
> silver
> gold
> platinum

D The higher a metal is in the reactivity series, the greater its tendency to form positive ions.

Circle the name of the metal in each word equation below that has the greater tendency to form a positive ion.

a zinc + lead nitrate → zinc nitrate + lead

b magnesium + copper sulfate → magnesium sulfate + copper

c tin + silver nitrate → tin nitrate + silver

E Write word equations for the displacement reactions below.

a magnesium reacting with zinc nitrate solution to make magnesium nitrate solution and zinc

_____

b lead reacting with silver nitrate solution to make lead nitrate solution and silver

_____

c magnesium reacting with iron chloride solution to make magnesium chloride solution and iron

_____

F The chemical equations below represent displacement reactions.

Balance the equations (if necessary – one is already balanced) and add state symbols. Do not change the formulae!

a $Mg + ZnCl_2 \rightarrow MgCl_2 + Zn$

b $Cu + AgNO_3 \rightarrow Cu(NO_3)_2 + Ag$

> **What you need to remember**
>
> In a displacement reaction, a _____ reactive metal displaces a _____ reactive metal from a _____ of its salt. The non-metals hydrogen and _____ are often included in the _____ series.

C5.3 Extracting metals

A Unreactive metals are found in the Earth as the metal itself.

Circle the names of **two** metals in the list below that can be found uncombined with other elements.

      copper   **gold**   **magnesium**   **sodium**

B Many metals occur in the Earth as oxides. Metals that are less reactive than carbon can be extracted from their oxides by heating with carbon.

Tick the metals that can be extracted from their oxides in this way.

Metal	✓ if it can be extracted from its oxide by heating with carbon
aluminium	
calcium	
copper	
iron	
lead	
magnesium	
sodium	
tin	

C Look at the word equation on the right: lead oxide + carbon → lead + carbon dioxide

In the word equation:

- circle in pencil the metal that is made
- circle in blue the substance that removes oxygen from the metal oxide
- circle in red the substance that is reduced
- circle in green the product that is not wanted.

D Write a word equation for each reaction described below.

a Zinc oxide reacts with carbon to make zinc and carbon dioxide.

_____

b Copper oxide reacts with carbon to make copper and carbon dioxide.

_____

c Iron oxide reacts with carbon to make iron and carbon dioxide.

_____

E Balance the chemical equations below. Do not change the formulae!

a PbO + C → Pb + CO_2

b ZnO + C → Zn + CO_2

c CuO + C → Cu + CO_2

d Fe_2O_3 + C → Fe + CO_2

What you need to remember

Gold and some other _____ metals can be found in the Earth as the metal itself. The metals _____ carbon in the reactivity series can be extracted from their oxides by heating with _____. Carbon removes the _____ from a metal oxide to form the metal and _____. In these reactions, the metal oxide is _____. Metals above carbon in the reactivity series _____ be extracted from their ores with carbon.

C5.4 Salts from metals

A What is a **salt**? Tick the best definition.

W a compound that includes sodium ions ☐

X a compound that includes chloride ions ☐

Y a compound in which the hydrogen in an acid is replaced by metal ions ☐

Z a compound in which the hydrogen in an acid is replaced by non-metal ions ☐

B All acid solutions contain hydrogen ions, H^+ (aq). Metals that are more reactive than hydrogen react with dilute acids.

Tick the metals that react with dilute acids.

Metal	✓ if the metal reacts with dilute acids
calcium	
copper	
gold	
iron	
lead	
magnesium	

Part of the reactivity series

potassium
sodium
calcium
magnesium
carbon
zinc
iron
lead
hydrogen
copper
silver
gold

C Circle the names of the metals that react violently with dilute acids.

copper   iron   lead   magnesium   potassium   sodium   zinc

D Draw lines to show which salts are formed from which acids, and the negative ions they contain.

Acid	Salts formed	Name of negative ion in the salt	Formula of negative ion in the salt
hydrochloric	sulfates	nitrate	Cl^-
sulfuric	chlorides	chloride	NO_3^-
nitric	nitrates	sulfate	SO_4^{2-}

E Fill in the gaps to complete the sentences below.

a Magnesium reacts with hydrochloric acid to make magnesium _____.

b Zinc reacts with _____ to make zinc sulfate.

c _____ reacts with hydrochloric acid to make iron _____

F Complete the word equations below.

a magnesium + sulfuric acid → magnesium _____ + hydrogen

b zinc + _____ acid → _____ chloride + _____

c _____ + sulfuric acid → iron _____ + _____

What you need to remember

You can make a salt by reacting a metal with an _____ . The reaction between a metal and an acid makes a salt _____ and _____ gas. You can then _____ the water to obtain _____ of the salt.

C5.5 Salts from insoluble bases

A Circle the correct **bold** words in the sentences below.

You can make a salt by reacting a base with an **alkali/acid**. Bases include **insoluble/soluble** metal oxides, such as copper oxide, and **insoluble/soluble** metal hydroxides. These reactions are **neutralisation/displacement** reactions. The products are a salt and **hydrogen/water**. Hydrochloric acid makes **chlorides/hydrochlorides**, sulfuric acid makes **sulfates/nitrates**, and nitric acid makes **sulfates/nitrates**.

B You can make different salts by choosing a suitable acid and base. Complete the table.

Acid	Base	Name of salt formed	Name of other product
hydrochloric acid	copper oxide		
sulfuric acid	magnesium oxide		
nitric acid		zinc nitrate	
	magnesium oxide	magnesium chloride	
		copper sulfate	

C Work out the formulae of the salts below. Use the formulae of the ions shown on the right. Remember, the sum of the charges on the ions in a salt add up to zero.

a magnesium sulfate _____ .

b sodium chloride _____

c sodium nitrate _____

d aluminium chloride _____

e zinc chloride _____

f sodium sulfate _____

g copper nitrate _____

h aluminium sulfate _____

Formulae of negative ions
chloride, Cl^-
sulfate, SO_4^{2-}
nitrate, NO_3^-

Formulae of positive ions
magnesium, Mg^{2+}
zinc, Zn^{2+}
copper, Cu^{2+}
sodium, Na^+
aluminium, Al^{3+}

D Write the letters of the steps below in the correct order to describe how to make copper sulfate from copper oxide and sulfuric acid.

Correct order: _____

T Use a spatula to add copper oxide powder to the sulfuric acid, a bit at a time, and warm gently.

U Filter the mixture and pour the filtrate into an evaporating dish.

V Measure out 25 cm³ of dilute sulfuric acid and pour it into a beaker.

W Leave the Petri dish at room temperature for a few days.

X Place the evaporating dish and its contents on a beaker of water. Place on a tripod and gauze and heat with a Bunsen burner.

Y Stop adding the copper oxide to the acid when the solid no longer dissolves when more copper oxide is added.

Z Stop heating when crystals start to appear around the edge of the solution. When cool, pour into a Petri dish.

E Balance the equations below. Do not change the formulae!

a $CuO + HCl \rightarrow CuCl_2 + H_2O$

b $ZnO + HCl \rightarrow ZnCl_2 + H_2O$

What you need to remember

When an _____ reacts with a base, there is a neutralisation reaction. The _____ of the reaction are a salt and water. The _____ of the charges on the ions in a salt always add up to _____ .

C5.6 Making more salts

A Draw a line to match each set of reactants to its products.

Reactants

| acid and metal |
| acid and insoluble base |
| acid and alkali |
| acid and carbonate |

Products

| salt and water |
| salt and hydrogen |
| salt, water, and carbon dioxide |

B How do you know when you have added enough reactant to react with an acid?

Tick one column next to each reactant to show how you know when you have added enough.

Reactant added to acid	How do you know you have added enough?	
	It will not fizz when you add more	Use an indicator
metal		
carbonate		
alkali		
insoluble base		

C

Name	Formula	State in the reaction
hydrochloric acid	HCl	in solution
sulfuric acid	H_2SO_4	in solution
nitric acid	HNO_3	in solution
water	H_2O	liquid
carbon dioxide	CO_2	gas
sodium hydroxide	NaOH	in solution

Name	Formula	State in the reaction
potassium hydroxide	KOH	in solution
calcium carbonate	$CaCO_3$	solid
copper carbonate	$CuCO_3$	solid
copper oxide	CuO	solid
copper nitrate	$Cu(NO_3)_2$	in solution
sodium chloride	NaCl	in solution

Write a balanced equation under each word equation. Use the formulae shown in the tables above. Include state symbols.

a hydrochloric acid + sodium hydroxide → sodium chloride + water

_____

b sulfuric acid + copper carbonate → copper oxide + water + carbon dioxide

_____

c nitric acid + copper carbonate → copper nitrate + water + carbon dioxide

_____

What you need to remember

An alkali reacts with an acid to make a salt and _____ . You need to use an _____ to find out how much alkali to add to a given volume of acid, and then _____ the experiment without the indicator to make a _____ of the salt. A carbonate reacts with an acid to make a _____ , water, and _____ _____ .

C5.7 Neutralisation and the pH scale

A Draw a line to match each word or phrase to its definition.

acid	This is a substance that is neither acidic nor alkaline.
alkali	This is a substance that produces hydrogen ions (H^+) in aqueous solution.
base	This is a soluble hydroxide. It contains hydroxide ions (OH^-).
neutral	This tells you how acidic or alkaline a substance is.
pH scale	This is any substance that can neutralise an acid.

B In the pH scale below:

● colour in green the pH of a neutral solution

● colour in red the pH of acidic solutions

● colour in purple the pH of alkaline solutions.

0	1	2	3	4	5	6	7	8	9	10	11	12	13	14

C Draw lines to make **six** correct sentences. Each sentence has one part from each column.

When you add an alkali to an acid	contains H^+ ions.
An alkaline solution	the pH increases.
When you add an acid to an alkali	the pH decreases.
An acid	a neutralisation reaction occurs.
	contains OH^- ions.

D A student poured a solution into a flask. She recorded the change in pH when she added a different solution from a burette.

Did the student add acid to alkali or did they add alkali to acid? Explain how you decided on your answer.

_____

_____

_____

_____

_____

_____

What you need to remember

_____ are substances that produce H^+(aq) ions when you add them to water. _____ are substances that neutralise acids. Alkalis are substances that produce _____ (aq) ions when you add them to _____ . The pH scale shows how acidic or _____ a solution is. Solutions with pH values _____ than 7 are acidic, solutions with pH values _____ than 7 are alkaline, and a solution of pH 7 is _____ .

C5 Practice questions

01 A student measures the pH of four solutions, **W, X, Y,** and **Z.** Her results are shown in **Table 1.**

Table 1

Solution	pH
W	1
X	4
Y	7
Z	12

01.1 Describe how you can use an indicator to measure the pH of a solution.
Include the names of the apparatus and the name of the indicator. [3 marks]

_____

_____

_____

01.2 Write the letter of the alkaline solution. [1 mark]

_____

01.3 Write the letter of the most acidic solution. [1 mark]

_____

01.4 Write the formula of one ion that must be present in solution **Z**. [1 mark]

_____

> **HINT** Decide whether solution Z is acidic or alkaline. You will then know which ion it contains, hydrogen ions or hydroxide ions.

02 Look at the equation below.
copper oxide + carbon →
                          copper + carbon dioxide

02.1 Name the substance in the equation that is reduced. [1 mark]

_____

02.2 Balance the equation below by writing one number on each dotted line. [2 marks]
.....$CuO(s) + C(s) \rightarrow$ ....$Cu(s) + CO_2(g)$

> **HINT** Never change a formula when you balance an equation.

03 A student makes copper sulfate crystals by reacting copper oxide with dilute sulfuric acid. Look at the outline of her method.

1. Add copper oxide powder to warm dilute sulfuric acid until no more copper oxide will dissolve.

2. Separate the undissolved copper oxide from the copper sulfate solution.

3. Remove water from the copper sulfate solution.

03.1 Write down the **two** missing state symbols in the equation for the reaction. [2 marks]
$CuO(s) + H_2SO_4(\_\_) \rightarrow CuSO_4(aq) + H_2O(\_\_)$

03.2 Describe how to carry out each step of the experiment. Give the names of the pieces of apparatus required. Include the names of the separation techniques. [6 marks]

> **HINT** Describe one step at a time. For each step, write down the names of the apparatus and separation techniques.

_____

_____

_____

_____

_____

_____

_____

_____

_____

_____

_____

_____

04 A student wanted to make zinc chloride crystals by reacting a metal with an acid.

04.1 Which acid should the student use?
Tick **one** box. [1 mark]

ethanoic acid ☐   nitric acid ☐

hydrochloric acid ☐   sulfuric acid ☐

> **HINT** Look at the names of the acids. Which one includes chloride ions?

04.2 The student placed some acid in a conical flask. He added zinc metal until no more would react. Then he filtered the resulting mixture.
Explain why the student filtered the mixture. [1 mark]

_____

_____

04.3 The student then wanted to remove the water from the solution. Which process did he use?
Tick **one** box. [1 mark]

filtration ☐   crystallisation ☐

neutralisation ☐   decomposition ☐

C5 Checklist

	Student Book	☺	😐	☹
I can describe how some common metals react with water.	5.1			
I can describe how some common metals react with dilute hydrochloric acid.	5.1			
I can use experimental results to deduce an order of reactivity of metals.	5.1			
I can explain reduction and oxidation in terms of loss or gain of oxygen.	5.1			
I can predict reactions of unfamiliar metals given information about their relative reactivity.	5.1			
I can use the reactivity series to predict displacement reactions.	5.2			
I can explain how the reactivity of a metal is related to the tendency of the metal to form its positive ion.	5.2			
I can evaluate and interpret information to describe how to extract different metals.	5.3			
I can identify substances that are oxidised or reduced in terms of gain or loss of oxygen.	5.3			
I can describe the reactions of magnesium, zinc, and iron with hydrochloric and sulfuric acids, and how to collect the salts formed.	5.4			
I can describe the reaction between an acid and a base.	5.5			
I can describe how to prepare pure, dry crystals of the salts formed in neutralisation reactions between acids and insoluble bases.	5.5			
I can predict the products from given reactants.	5.5			
I can use the formulae of common ions to work out the formulae of salts.	5.5			
I can describe the reactions of acids with alkalis and predict the products formed.	5.6			
I can describe the reactions of acids with carbonates and predict the products formed.	5.6			
I can describe how to make a pure, dry sample of a named soluble salt.	5.6			
I can explain what makes a solution acidic or alkaline.	5.7			
I can describe how to use universal indicator or another wide-range indicator to measure the approximate pH of a solution.	5.7			
I can describe how to use the pH scale to identify acidic or alkaline solutions.	5.7			
I can describe how to investigate pH changes when a strong acid neutralises a strong alkali.	5.7			

C6.1 Introduction to electrolysis

A Draw a line to match each word to its definition.

electrolysis	a positive electrode
electrolyte	describes a substance that is unreactive
anode	using electricity to break down a substance
cathode	a negative electrode
inert	a compound that is broken down by electricity

B Molten zinc chloride can be broken down by electrolysis. The diagram shows the electrolysis of molten zinc chloride.

Write the labels below in the correct spaces.

anode   electrolyte   zinc metal   chlorine gas

liquid zinc chloride   cathode

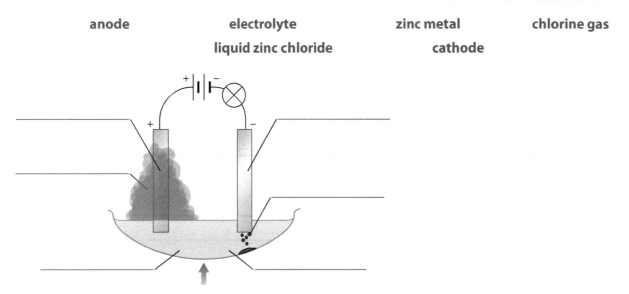

C Circle the correct **bold** words in the sentences below.

When zinc chloride is **liquid/solid** its ions are free to move. **Positively/negatively** charged zinc ions (Zn^{2+}) move towards the negative electrode (the **anode/cathode**) and **positively/negatively** charged chloride ions (Cl^-) ions move towards the positive electrode (the **anode/cathode**). When the ions react at the electrodes, they **gain/lose** their charge and become elements.

It can be easier to electrolyse an aqueous solution of a salt, rather than melt it at a very **high/low** temperature.

What you need to remember

Electrolysis uses _____ to break down a compound. Ionic compounds are only electrolysed when their ions are free to _____ , so the compound needs to be in the _____ state, or dissolved in _____ . In electrolysis, positive ions move to the _____ electrode (_____) and negative ions move to the _____ electrode (_____).

C6.2 Changes at the electrodes

A Choose words from the list to complete the sentences below.

oxygen	negative	hydrogen	electrode	chloride
hydroxide	molecules	sodium	gas	anode

a In water, a few water _____ split up to form ions.

b A water molecule splits up to make hydrogen ions (H⁺) and _____ ions (OH⁻).

c Sodium chloride solution has two types of positive ion, _____ ions and hydrogen ions.

d Sodium chloride has two types of negative ion, _____ ions and hydroxide ions.

e In the electrolysis of sodium chloride, two types of ion are attracted to the negative _____ (cathode).

f In the electrolysis of sodium chloride, the two types of ion that are attracted to the cathode are sodium ions and _____ ions.

g Hydrogen is less reactive than sodium, so hydrogen _____ is produced at the cathode.

h In the electrolysis of sodium chloride, two types of _____ ion are attracted to the anode.

i In the electrolysis of sodium chloride, the two types of ion that are attracted to the _____ are chloride ions and hydroxide ions.

j Chlorine is produced at the anode. For solutions without halide ions, _____ is produced at the anode.

B Tick the statements that are true for the electrolysis of copper bromide solution.

Statement	✓ if true
Positive copper ions (Cu^{2+}) are attracted to the cathode.	
Copper metal is deposited at the anode.	
Negative bromide ions (Br^-) are attracted to the anode.	
Bromine forms at the cathode.	

Write corrected versions of the **two** statements that are false.

_____

_____

C Only metals that are below hydrogen in the reactivity series can be deposited from their aqueous solutions by electrolysis.

Circle the solutions that would deposit a metal at the cathode. The reactivity series in Topic C5.4 will help you.

copper chloride	potassium chloride	silver nitrate	iron chloride

What you need to remember

In electrolysis, ions move towards the charged rods called _____ . In the electrolysis of an aqueous solution, either _____ or the metal can be produced at the _____ . The metal is only produced if it is _____ reactive than hydrogen, such as copper. At the anode, _____ is usually produced unless the electrolyte is a solution of a halide such as a chloride, _____ , or iodide.

A Metals below carbon in the reactivity series can be extracted from their oxides by heating with carbon. Metals above carbon are extracted by electrolysis.

Tick to show how the metals in the table can be extracted from their compounds.

Metal	✓ if it can be extracted from its oxide by heating with carbon	✓ if it is extracted by electrolysis
aluminium		
calcium		
iron		
magnesium		
zinc		

Part of the reactivity series

potassium
sodium
calcium
magnesium
aluminium

carbon

zinc
iron
lead
copper
gold

B Aluminium is extracted from its oxide by electrolysis. The diagram shows the cell that is used for this process.

Write the letter for each label below in the correct spaces.

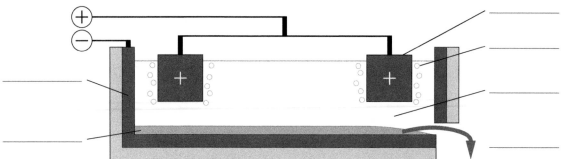

U carbon anode (positive electrode)

V carbon cathode (negative electrode)

W mixture of molten aluminium oxide and cryolite

X liquid aluminium

Y carbon dioxide

Z molten aluminium is tapped or siphoned off from the cell

C Complete the equations.

a The overall equation for the electrolysis cell is:

aluminium oxide → aluminium + _____

$2Al_2O_3(\text{\_\_\_}) \rightarrow \text{\_\_\_} Al(l) + 3O_2(g)$

b The equation that occurs at the hot carbon anode is:

carbon + oxygen → _____ _____

$C(\text{\_\_\_}) + O_2(\text{\_\_\_}) \rightarrow CO_2(\text{\_\_\_})$

What you need to remember

Aluminium is extracted from aluminium oxide by _____ . First, aluminium oxide is mixed with _____ to lower the melting temperature. When electricity is passed through the cell, _____ forms at the negative electrode (_____) and oxygen forms at the _____ electrode (anode). The oxygen reacts with the hot _____ anodes, forming carbon _____ gas. This means that the _____ must be replaced often.

A The diagram shows an electrolysis cell you might use at school. The electrodes are inert. This means that they are made from an unreactive substance, for example graphite. Then the electrodes do not react with the electrolyte or the products made in electrolysis.

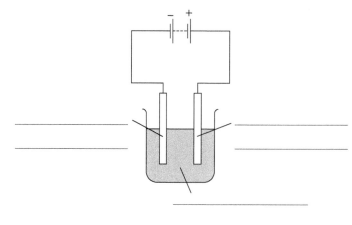

Write the labels below in the correct spaces.

electrolyte   anode (positive electrode)

cathode (negative electrode)

B Circle the correct **bold** words in the sentences below.

When a molten ionic compound such as lead bromide is electrolysed, the **metal/non-metal** (lead) is produced at the negative electrode (**cathode/anode**). The **metal/non-metal** (bromine) is produced at the positive electrode (**cathode/anode**).

In an aqueous solution, a few water molecules break down to make hydrogen and **oxide/hydroxide** ions:
$H_2O(l) \rightarrow H^+(aq) + OH^-(aq)$

The products of electrolysis depend on the elements involved.

- At the **positive/negative** electrode (cathode), hydrogen is produced if the metal is **more/less** reactive than hydrogen.
- At the **positive/negative** electrode (anode), **oxygen/hydrogen** is produced unless the solution contains chloride, bromide, or iodide ions.

C Predict the products of electrolysis of the solutions below. Use the reactivity series to help you.

Substance	Molten or in solution?	Products of electrolysis	
		at cathode (–)	at anode (+)
lead bromide	molten		bromine
zinc chloride	molten	zinc	
zinc chloride	solution	hydrogen	
sodium chloride	solution		
potassium bromide	solution		
copper sulfate	solution		
silver nitrate	solution		

Part of the reactivity series

potassium
sodium
calcium
magnesium
zinc
iron
lead

hydrogen

copper
silver

What you need to remember

When you electrolyse an aqueous solution:

- at the negative electrode (cathode), _____ is produced if the metal is more reactive than hydrogen
- at the positive electrode (anode), _____ is produced unless the solution contains halide ions, in which case the _____ is produced.

C6 Practice questions

01 **Figure 1** shows the apparatus for an electrolysis experiment.

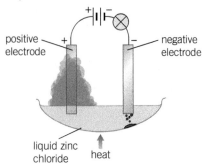

Figure 1

01.1 The electrodes in the experiment are inert. Define the word *inert*. [1 mark]

_____

01.2 Predict the **one** substance formed at each electrode.

Positive electrode (anode):

_____ [1 mark]

Negative electrode (cathode):

_____ [1 mark]

01.3 The information in the box describes some of the hazards of the gas produced at the anode.

> The gas causes severe lung damage if breathed in. It irritates the eyes and skin. It may trigger an asthma attack.

A teacher is demonstrating the electrolysis experiment in **Figure 1**. Suggest **two** safety precautions, in addition to wearing eye protection, that she should take to minimise the risks from these hazards to her students. [1 mark]

_____

_____

HINT Where might the teacher do the experiment? What might she ask her students before she starts?

02 A student is investigating the electrolysis of copper sulfate solution.
She wants to find out about the factors that affect the mass of copper deposited. **Figure 2** shows her apparatus.

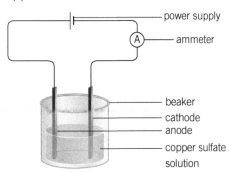

Figure 2

02.1 Name the electrolyte. [1 mark]

_____

02.2 Name the gas released at the anode. [1 mark]

_____

HINT In the electrolysis of a solution, oxygen is released unless the solution includes chloride, bromide, or iodide ions.

02.3 Explain why the mass of the cathode will increase. [2 marks]

_____

_____

02.4 The student obtains the results shown in **Table 1**.

Table 1

Current in A	Mass of copper deposited in g
0.4	0.08
0.6	0.12
0.8	0.16
1.0	0.20
1.2	0.24

Suggest the question the student is investigating. [1 mark]

_____

_____

HINT Try writing a question in this form:
What happens to the _____ as the student increases the _____?

02.5 On **Figure 3**, below:

- plot the data from the table. The first two have been done for you.
- draw a line of best fit. [3 marks]

HINT Read the scale carefully as you plot the points.

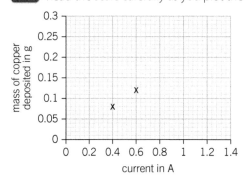

Figure 3

02.6 Write a conclusion for the investigation. [1 mark]

_____

_____

HINT Your conclusion should answer the scientific question in **02.4**.

C6 Checklist

	Student Book	☺	☺	☹
I can describe what happens in electrolysis.	6.1			
I can write down the types of substances that can be electrolysed.	6.1			
I can predict the products of electrolysis of molten ionic compounds.	6.1			
I can describe simply what happens to the ions during electrolysis.	6.2			
I can explain how water affects the products of electrolysis.	6.2			
I can explain why some metals are extracted with carbon and others by electrolysis.	6.3			
I can describe the process of extracting aluminium from its ore.	6.3			
I can predict the products of electrolysis of an aqueous solution.	6.4			
I can describe how to investigate the electrolysis of a solution using inert electrodes.	6.4			

C7.1 Exothermic and endothermic reactions

A Chemical reactions transfer energy to or from the surroundings.

Draw lines to match each term to its description and temperature change.

Term	Description	Temperature change
exothermic reaction	a reaction in which energy is transferred from the reacting substances to the surroundings	As the reaction happens, the temperature of the reaction mixture decreases.
endothermic reaction	a reaction in which energy is transferred from the surroundings to the reacting substances	As the reaction happens, the temperature of the reaction mixture increases.

B When methane gas burns, it reacts with oxygen in the air.

Tick the statements that are true for this reaction:

methane + oxygen → carbon dioxide + water
$CH_4(g)$ + $2O_2(g)$ → $CO_2(g)$ + $2H_2O(l)$ energy transferred to surroundings = 890 kJ/mol

Statement	✓ if true
The products have a lower energy content than the reactants.	
The total energy content of the methane and oxygen is more than the total energy content of the carbon dioxide and water.	
During the reaction, the temperature of the surroundings decreases.	

Write a corrected version of the **one** statement that is false.

_____

C A student mixed some pairs of reactants, and reactions took place. She measured the temperatures before and after the reaction.

a Complete the table.

b Colour the exothermic reactions red, and the endothermic reactions blue.

Reactants	Temperature before reaction in °C	Temperature after reaction in °C	Temperature change in °C
sodium hydroxide solution and dilute nitric acid	19	45	
copper sulfate solution and magnesium powder	21		14
sulfuric acid and potassium hydroxide solution	21	51	
citric acid powder and sodium hydrogencarbonate powder	22	8	

What you need to remember

Energy is conserved in chemical reactions. It is neither created nor _____ . An exothermic reaction

transfers energy _____ the reacting substances _____ the surroundings.

An _____ reaction transfers energy from the surroundings to the reacting substances.

C7.2 Using energy transfers from reactions

A Tick to show whether each type of reaction is exothermic or endothermic.

Type of reaction and example	✓ if exothermic	✓ if endothermic
combustion methane + oxygen → carbon dioxide + water		
thermal decomposition copper carbonate → copper oxide + carbon dioxide		

B Exothermic and endothermic reactions can be useful.

Draw lines to match each use to one statement in each column.

Use	**Exothermic or endothermic?**	**Does it heat or cool the surroundings?**
sports injury packs	endothermic	heats the surroundings
hand warmers	exothermic	cools the surroundings

C The diagram shows a self-heating can.

Different people make different comments about the self-heating can.

- Circle the advantages in green.
- Circle the disadvantages in red.
- Circle comments that are neither advantages nor disadvantages in black.

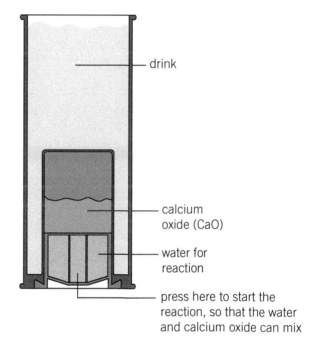

drink

calcium oxide (CaO)

water for reaction

press here to start the reaction, so that the water and calcium oxide can mix

Catherine   The heating chamber takes about a third of the volume of the can.

Barney   I can have a hot drink whenever and wherever I want.

Sarah   The equation for the exothermic reaction is: calcium oxide + water → calcium hydroxide

Edward   It took about 10 years for scientists to develop the self-heating can.

Mary   When you press the button, it breaks a seal between the water and calcium oxide so that they can react. You have to press very hard.

What you need to remember

_____ reactions are used in hand warmers and self-heating cans. _____ reactions are useful for cold packs to treat sports injuries.

C7.3 Reaction profiles

A A reaction profile shows the energy levels of the reactants and products. The diagram below shows the reaction profile for an exothermic reaction.

Write the labels below in the correct boxes.

reactants   **products**   **progress of reaction**   **energy**   **energy change**

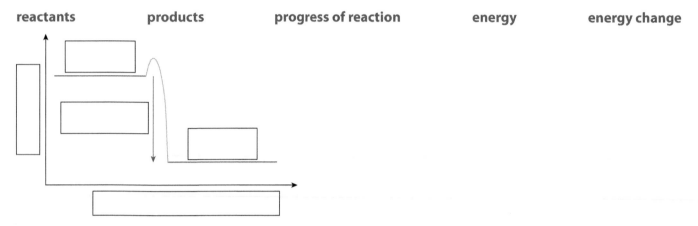

B Draw a reaction profile for an endothermic reaction in the box below. Add labels to your diagram. You can use the same labels as for activity **A**.

C Look at the diagram below. Which arrow represents the **activation** energy?

Circle the correct letter: **P   Q   R   S   T**

C7 Practice questions

01 A student measures the temperature change when she dissolves different substances in water.

01.1 Figure 1 shows the student's apparatus.

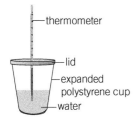

Figure 1

Explain why she uses a polystyrene cup with a lid, and not a glass beaker. [1 mark]

_____

01.2 The student's results are in **Table 1**.

Table 1

Substance added to water	Temperature of water before adding substance in °C	Temperature of mixture after substance has dissolved in °C	Temperature change in °C
ammonium chloride	20	16	− 4
ammonium nitrate	20	14	
copper sulfate (anhydrous)	20	27	+ 7
lithium chloride	20	26	+ 6

Calculate the temperature change when ammonium nitrate dissolves in water. [1 mark]

_____ °C

01.3 Name the **two** substances in the table that dissolve in water in endothermic changes. [1 mark]

_____ and _____

01.4 Name the **two** substances in the table that transfer energy to the surroundings when they dissolve in water. [1 mark]

_____ and _____

02 A student carries out an investigation to answer this question:

When dilute hydrochloric acid reacts with metals, which metal–acid reaction transfers most energy to the surroundings?

He follows the procedure below.

1. Pour hydrochloric acid into a polystyrene cup.

2. Measure the temperature of the acid.

3. Add a piece of magnesium ribbon.

4. Measure the highest temperature reached.

5. Repeat with zinc, iron, and copper instead of the magnesium ribbon.

02.1 Name the apparatus the student should use to measure temperature. [1 mark]

_____

02.2 Here is a list of variables in the investigation:

- metal
- temperature change
- concentration of acid
- volume of acid
- amount of metal.

Identify the independent variable in the list above. [1 mark]

_____

02.3 Identify **three** variables the student should keep constant. [3 marks]

_____

_____

_____

02.4 The student designs a table for his results (**Table 2**).

Table 2

	Temperature of acid before reaction in °C		Temperature change in °C
magnesium			
zinc			
iron			
copper			

Write the **two** missing column headings in the table. [2 marks]

03 **Figure 2** shows the reaction profile for a chemical reaction.

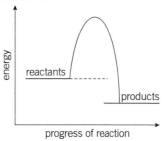

Figure 2

Explain how the reaction profile shows that the reaction is exothermic. [2 marks]

_____

_____

C7 Checklist

	Student Book	☺	☺	☹
I can write down that energy cannot be created or destroyed in a chemical reaction.	7.1			
I can describe energy transfers to or from the surroundings in exothermic and endothermic reactions.	7.1			
I can give examples of exothermic and endothermic reactions.	7.1			
I can use temperature change data to distinguish between exothermic and endothermic reactions.	7.1			
I can describe how to carry out an investigation into energy changes in chemical reactions.	7.1			
I can describe how you can make use of the energy from exothermic reactions.	7.2			
I can describe how you can use the cooling effect of endothermic reactions.	7.2			
I can evaluate uses and applications of exothermic and endothermic reactions given appropriate information.	7.2			
I can draw simple reaction profiles for exothermic and endothermic reactions, including the activation energy.	7.3			
I can write down a definition of activation energy.	7.3			
I can use reaction profiles to identify reactions as exothermic or endothermic.	7.3			

C8.1 Rate of reaction

A You can use either of the equations below to find the rate of a chemical reaction.

Complete the equations by writing **one** phrase in each box.

$$\text{mean rate of reaction} = \frac{\text{quantity of reactant used}}{\boxed{}}$$

$$\boxed{} = \frac{\text{quantity of product formed}}{\text{time taken}}$$

B You can use different methods to measure the rate of a chemical reaction.

Draw lines to match each method to its apparatus and graph.

Method	**Apparatus**	**Graph**
measuring the decreasing mass of a reaction mixture	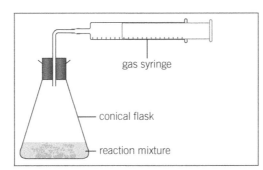	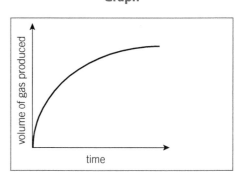
measuring the increasing volume of gas given off	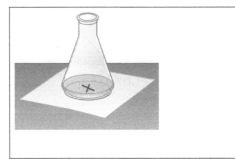	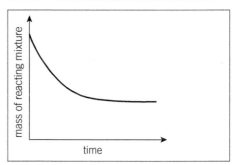
measuring the decreasing amount of light passing through a reaction mixture	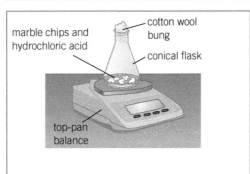	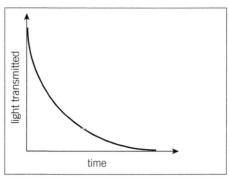

What you need to remember

You can find out the rate of a reaction by monitoring *either* the amount of _____
used up over time, *or* the amount of _____ made over time. You then need to draw
a _____ to display the results. The _____ of the line at any time on the
graph tells you the rate of reaction at that time. The _____ the slope, the faster the reaction.

C8.2 Collision theory and surface area

A Circle the correct **bold** words to complete the definitions below.

The activation energy is the **minimum/maximum** amount of energy that particles must have in order to react.

Collision theory states that a chemical reaction can only happen when reacting particles come together. They must collide with enough **temperature/energy** to cause a reaction.

B Whether a reaction is likely to happen depends on the movement of the particles.

Tick the correct column next to each change.

Change	✓ if this change makes reactions more likely to happen	✓ if this change makes reactions less likely to happen
increasing the energy that particles have when they collide		
decreasing the energy that particles have when they collide		
increasing the frequency of collisions between reacting particles		

C Chao adds 3 g of calcium carbonate to dilute hydrochloric acid. He repeats the experiment using different sized pieces of calcium carbonate, but keeps everything else the same (including the mass of calcium carbonate). The sizes are:

powder   **small lumps**   **big lumps**

- Circle in red the size that reacts most quickly.
- Circle in green the size with the greatest surface area.

D Chao obtained the results in the table below.

Size of calcium carbonate	Decrease in mass of reacting mixture in g	Time for this decrease in mass to occur in s
powder	2.0	50
small lumps	2.0	150
big lumps	2.0	200

Use the equation below to calculate the mean rate of reaction for calcium carbonate powder and big lumps of calcium carbonate:

$$\text{mean rate of reaction} = \frac{\text{mass of reactants used up in g}}{\text{time in s}}$$

Powder $\text{mean rate of reaction} = \dfrac{2.0 \text{ g}}{50 \text{ s}}$

$$= \boxed{} \text{ g/s}$$

Big lumps $\text{mean rate of reaction} = \dfrac{\boxed{} \text{ g}}{\boxed{} \text{ s}}$

$$= \boxed{} \text{ g/s}$$

What you need to remember

Particles must collide, with enough _____, in order to react. The _____

energy that particles must have in order to react is the _____ energy. The rate of a

chemical reaction _____ as the surface area of a solid increases. This is because the

frequency of _____ between reacting particles increases.

C8.3 The effect of temperature

A Reaction rate increases as the temperature of a reaction mixture increases.

Write the letters of the statements below in the best order to explain one reason for this.

Order: _____

V This increases the rate of reaction.

W When you heat a substance, energy is transferred to its particles.

X For this reason, the particles collide more often.

Y This means that there are more chances for the particles to react.

Z This makes particles in solutions and gases move around faster.

B Reaction rate increases as the temperature of a reaction mixture increases.

Circle the correct **bold** words in the sentences below to explain a second reason for this.

Particles that move faster have **more/less** energy. This means that collisions between them are **more/less** energetic. As temperature increases, a **smaller/higher** proportion of collisions results in reaction in a given time. This is because a **smaller/higher** proportion of particles have energy that is **greater/less** than the activation energy.

C Zac asks the scientific question: 'How does temperature affect the rate of reaction of magnesium with hydrochloric acid?' He adds magnesium ribbon to dilute hydrochloric acid, and measures the time for the fizzing to stop. The table lists some variables in the investigation.

Tick **one** column next to each variable.

Variable	✓ if this is... the independent variable (the one that he should deliberately change)	✓ if this is... the dependent variable (the one that changes as a result of the independent variable changing)	✓ if this is... a control variable
temperature			
volume of acid			
concentration of acid			
length of magnesium ribbon			
time for fizzing to stop			

D The table shows Zac's results.

Temperature in °C	Time for fizzing to stop in s
10	160
20	82
30	38
40	20
50	10

a Circle in red the temperature at which the magnesium fizzes for the longest time.

b Circle in green the temperature at which the rate of reaction is quickest.

c How long would it take for the fizzing to stop at 60 °C? Circle the time below that is the best prediction.

1 s   5 s   15 s   20 s

What you need to remember

As temperature increases, the rate of reaction _____ . This is because increasing the temperature _____ the frequency of collisions between particles, and makes the particles collide with more _____ .

A Draw lines to make **12** correct sentences. Each sentence has one part from each column.

The higher the concentration of reactants in solution	the shorter the time for the reaction to finish.
	the less frequent the collisions.
	the faster the rate.
The lower the concentration of reactants in solution	the greater the number of reactant particles moving around in a given volume.
	the slower the rate.
The higher the pressure of reacting gases	the longer the time for the reaction to finish.
	the more frequent the collisions.
	the smaller the number of reactant particles moving around in a given volume.

B A student measures the time for the cross to disappear when sodium thiosulfate reacts with hydrochloric acid:

sodium thiosulfate + hydrochloric acid → sodium chloride + water + sulfur dioxide + sulfur

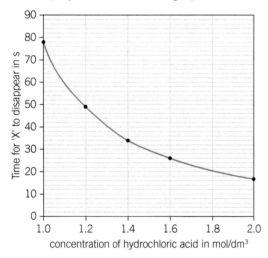

She displays her results on a graph. Circle the correct **bold** words in the sentences below.

To make the investigation fair, the student needed to keep the **temperature/concentration** the same and the **volumes/concentrations** of the reactants the same each time.

The time for the 'X' to disappear is shortest when the acid concentration is **2.0/1.0** mol/dm³. It is at this concentration that the reaction rate is **slowest/fastest**. The graph shows that as the acid concentration increases, the rate **increases/decreases**. This is because, at higher concentrations, there are **more/fewer** particles in a given volume of solution and so collisions are **more/less** frequent.

> **What you need to remember**
>
> Increasing the concentration of reactants in solution increases the frequency of _____
>
> between particles, and so _____ the rate of reaction. Increasing the pressure of reacting
>
> gases _____ the frequency of collisions, and so _____ the rate of reaction.

C8.5 The effect of catalysts

A Catalysts are very useful in industry.

Tick the statements about catalysts that are true.

Statement	✓ if true
Catalysts increase the rate of chemical reactions.	
Catalysts are used up in reactions.	
A catalyst provides a different pathway for a reaction with a higher activation energy.	
A catalyst increases the frequency of collisions between reactant particles.	
When writing a chemical equation, you should not include the catalyst as one of the reactants.	

Write corrected versions of the **two** statements that are false.

_____

_____

_____

B Catalysts affect the reaction profile. On the reaction profile below:

● draw a red arrow to show the activation energy without a catalyst

● draw a blue arrow to show the activation energy with a catalyst.

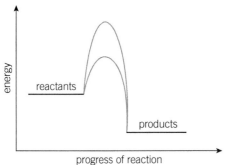

C A student is investigating the reaction shown in this equation:

hydrogen peroxide → water + oxygen

She adds three catalysts to separate samples of hydrogen peroxide solution. She measures the time for 20 cm³ of oxygen to form. Her results are in the table.

Catalyst	Time for 20 cm³ of oxygen to form in s
liver	10
celery	15
manganese(IV) oxide	18

Complete the sentences below.

The reaction with the _____ catalyst has the highest rate. This shows that the most effective catalyst for the reaction is _____. The least effective catalyst is _____.

What you need to remember

A catalyst _____ up a chemical reaction, but is not itself used up in the reaction. Different reactions need _____ catalysts. In industrial processes, catalysts are used to _____ reaction rates and reduce the _____ of the process, making it more profitable.

C8.6 Reversible reactions

A Tick the statements about reversible reactions that are true.

Statement	✓ if true
A reversible reaction can go in two directions.	
In an equation for a reversible reaction, the substances on the left of the $\rightleftharpoons$ symbol are called reactants.	
Indicators cannot undergo reversible reactions.	
Hydrated copper sulfate has no water of crystallisation.	
In a reversible reaction, the substances on the left of the $\rightleftharpoons$ symbol are called the products.	
Hydrated copper sulfate forms anhydrous copper sulfate when water is added to it.	
In a reversible reaction, the reactants react together to form products.	
In a reversible reaction, the products react together to form reactants.	

Write corrected versions of the **four** statements that are false.

_____

_____

_____

_____

_____

_____

B The reaction below is reversible.

ammonium chloride $\rightleftharpoons$ ammonia + hydrogen chloride

$$NH4Cl(s) \rightleftharpoons NH3(g) + HCl(g)$$

Complete the gaps in the sentences below. Use the word and symbol equations above to help you.

a The $\rightleftharpoons$ symbol shows that the reaction is _____ .

b The products of the reaction are _____ and hydrogen chloride.

c In this reaction, ammonium chloride is the _____ .

d When you heat ammonium chloride, it decomposes to make ammonia and hydrogen _____ .

e When a mixture of ammonia gas and hydrogen chloride gas cools, the gases react to make _____ chloride.

f If you heat ammonium chloride in the lab, you must wear _____ protection.

What you need to remember

In a reversible reaction, the _____ of the reaction can react to make the original _____ .
You can use the $\rightleftharpoons$ sign to show a _____ reaction.

C8.7 Energy and reversible reactions

A The equation shows a general reversible reaction:

W + X ⇌ Y + Z

The reaction that makes **Y** and **Z** is exothermic.

Tick the boxes to show which of the following statements must be true.

S The reaction that makes **W** and **X** is exothermic. ☐

T The reaction that makes **W** and **X** is endothermic. ☐

U The reaction that makes **Y** and **Z** transfers energy from the surroundings to the reaction mixture. ☐

V The reaction that makes **W** and **X** transfers energy from the reaction mixture to the surroundings. ☐

B A reaction transfers 860 kJ of energy from the reacting mixture to the surroundings.

How much energy is transferred from the surroundings to the reaction mixture in the reverse reaction?

_____ kJ

C Blue copper sulfate crystals include water of crystallisation. You can remove the water of crystallisation by heating to make a white powder and water. The reaction is reversible.

hydrated copper(II) sulfate ⇌ **anhydrous** copper(II) sulfate + water

$$CuSO_4.5H_2O \quad \rightleftharpoons \quad CuSO_4 \quad + \quad 5H_2O$$

- Circle in blue the name and formula of the reactant in the equation above.
- Circle in pencil the name and formula of the white powder.
- Circle in red the names and formulae of the two products.
- Circle in green the symbol that shows the reaction is reversible.
- The reaction that makes anhydrous copper sulfate is endothermic.
  Draw a big blue arrow to show the direction of the endothermic reaction.
- The reaction that makes hydrated copper sulfate is exothermic.
  Draw a big red arrow to show the direction of the exothermic reaction.

What you need to remember

In reversible reactions, the reaction in one direction is exothermic and the reaction in the other direction

is _____ . The amount of energy transferred from the reacting mixture to the

_____ in one direction is _____ to the amount of energy transferred

_____ the surroundings _____ the reacting mixture when the reaction

goes in the opposite direction.

C8.8 Dynamic equilibrium

A Which statement about **equilibrium** is true?

Tick **one** answer.

O At equilibrium, there is no change in the amounts of reactants and products. ☐
P At equilibrium, the amounts of products do not change but the amounts of reactants do change. ☐
Q At equilibrium, the amounts of reactants do not change but the amounts of products do change. ☐
R At equilibrium, the amounts of reactants are increasing and the amounts of products are decreasing. ☐

B Which statement about equilibrium is true?

Tick **one** answer.

S At equilibrium, the rate of the forward reaction is greater than the rate of the reverse reaction. ☐
T At equilibrium, the rate of the forward reaction is less than the rate of the reverse reaction. ☐
U At equilibrium, the rate of the forward reaction is equal to the rate of the reverse reaction. ☐
V At equilibrium, the reactants form products faster than the products re-form the reactants. ☐

C In chemistry, what is a closed system?

Tick the best answer.

W a system in which products only can get out ☐
X a system in which no products can get in ☐
Y a system in which no reactants can get in ☐
Z a system in which no reactants or products can get in or out ☐

D The graph below shows how the rates of the forward and backward reactions change as a reversible reaction is reaching equilibrium.

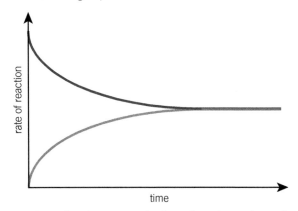

- In red, colour over the line that shows how the rate of the forward reaction changes with time.
- In blue, colour over the line that shows how the rate of the reverse reaction changes with time.
- Draw a cross (X) to show the time when equilibrium is reached.

What you need to remember

In a reversible reaction, the products can react to re-form the original _____ . Reactants and products cannot enter or leave a _____ system. In a closed system a reversible reaction can reach _____ . At equilibrium the rate of the _____ reaction is equal to the rate of the reverse reaction. The _____ of reactants and products do not change.

01 A student adds hydrochloric acid to magnesium ribbon in the apparatus shown in **Figure 1**.

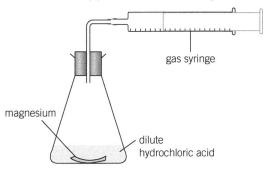

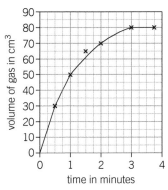

Figure 1

One of the products of the reaction is hydrogen gas. Every minute, the student records the volume of hydrogen gas in the gas syringe. **Figure 2** is a graph of the results.

Figure 2

01.1 Which description best describes how the volume of gas changes with time?

Tick **one** box. [1 mark]

The volume of gas increases quickly. ☐

The volume of gas increases slowly at first, and then more quickly. ☐

The volume of gas increases quickly at first, and then more slowly. ☐

The volume of gas increases slowly. ☐

01.2 Use data from the graph in **Figure 2** and the equation below to calculate the mean rate of reaction in the first minute. [2 marks]

$$\text{mean rate of reaction} = \frac{\text{volume of gas in cm}^3}{\text{time in minutes}}$$

rate of reaction = _____ cm³/minute

HINT The graph shows that the volume of gas produced in the first minute is 50 cm³.

01.3 Add a curved line to the graph to show how the volume of gas might change with time if the student did the investigation at a higher temperature. [2 marks]

02 A student reacts small lumps of calcium carbonate with dilute hydrochloric acid.

Figure 3 shows her apparatus.

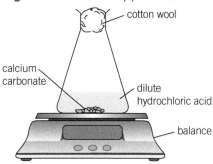

Figure 3

02.1 The equation below shows the reactants and products in the reaction.

$$2HCl + CaCO_3 \rightarrow CaCl_2 + CO_2 + H_2O$$

Complete the equation below to show the state of each reactant and product at room temperature. [2 marks]

$$2HCl(\underline{}) + CaCO_3(\underline{}) \rightarrow$$
$$CaCl_2(\underline{}) + CO_2(\underline{}) + H_2O(\underline{})$$

02.2 Name the salt formed in the reaction. [1 mark]

_____

02.3 The student records the mass of carbon dioxide produced by the end of each minute. The results are in **Table 1**.

Table 1

Time in minutes	Mass of carbon dioxide produced since the start in g
0	0.00
1	1.10
2	1.40
3	1.56
4	1.60
5	1.60

Plot the data in the table on **Figure 4** below. The first two points have been plotted for you. [2 marks]

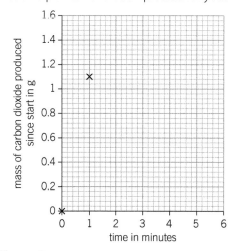

Figure 4

02.4 Draw a smooth curve on your graph. [1 mark]

C8 Checklist

	Student Book	☺	☺	☹
I can write down the meaning of the term *rate of chemical reaction*.	8.1			
I can describe how to collect data on the rate of a chemical reaction.	8.1			
I can calculate the mean rate of a reaction.	8.1			
I can write down the factors that can affect the rate of a chemical reaction.	8.2			
I can use collision theory to explain the effect of surface area on reaction rate.	8.2			
I can describe how increasing the temperature affects reaction rate.	8.3			
I can use the collision theory to explain how increasing temperature affects reaction rate.	8.3			
I can describe how increasing the concentration of reactants in solution affects the rate of reaction.	8.4			
I can explain why increasing the concentration of reactants in solution affects the rate of reaction.	8.4			
I can describe how increasing the pressure of reacting gases affects the rate of reaction.	8.4			
I can explain why increasing the pressure of reacting gases affects the rate of reaction.	8.4			
I can write down what a catalyst is.	8.5			
I can explain why catalysts are important in industry.	8.5			
I can write down what a reversible reaction is.	8.6			
I can write down an equation to represent a reversible reaction using the symbol $\rightleftharpoons$.	8.6			
I can describe the energy transfers between the reactions and the surroundings in reversible reactions.	8.7			
I can describe how a reversible reaction in a closed system can be 'at equilibrium'.	8.8			

C9.1 Hydrocarbons

A Draw a line to match each word to its definition.

mixture	a compound made up of hydrogen and carbon atoms only
hydrocarbon	a process used to separate a liquid from a mixture by evaporation followed by condensation
fractions	hydrocarbons with the general formula C_nH_{2n+2}. The first four are methane, ethane, propane, and butane.
distillation	two or more substances that are mixed together but that are not joined together
alkanes	a hydrocarbon that has single covalent bonds only between its carbon atoms
saturated hydrocarbon	hydrocarbons with similar boiling points that have been separated from crude oil

B Crude oil provides us with useful fuels.

Circle the correct **bold** words in the sentences below.

Crude oil is a **finite/infinite** resource. It is the remains of ancient living things, mainly plankton, that were buried in **coal/mud**. Crude oil is a mixture of **a few/many** compounds, mostly **hydroxides/hydrocarbons**. Most of the hydrocarbons in crude oil are **alkalis/alkanes**.

C Alkanes are a group of saturated hydrocarbons.

Complete the table.

Name of alkane	Molecular formula	Displayed formula
methane		H—C—H (with H above and H below the central C)
	C_2H_6	
propane		H—C—C—C—H (with H atoms above and below each C)
	C_4H_{10}	

D All alkanes have the general formula C_nH_{2n+2}.

Circle the formulae of the substances that are alkanes in the list below.

C_3H_8 C_5H_{12} C_6H_{12} C_7H_{16}

What you need to remember

Crude oil is a mixture of many different _____ . Most of the compounds in _____ oil are hydrocarbons. A hydrocarbon is a compound made up of _____ and carbon atoms _____ . Alkanes are saturated hydrocarbons, which means they have only _____ covalent bonds between their carbon atoms. The _____ formula of an alkane is C_nH_{2n+2}.

A Complete the table to compare the properties of two alkanes with molecules of different sizes.

Alkane	Boiling point	Viscosity	Flammability
C_5H_{12}		less viscous	
$C_{12}H_{26}$	higher		

B Crude oil is a mixture of hydrocarbons. Some of the properties of these hydrocarbons depend on the size of their molecules.

Circle the correct **bold** words in the sentences below.

The longer the hydrocarbon molecule, the **lower/higher** the boiling point of the hydrocarbon. The longer the molecule, the **less/more** flammable it is and the **less/more** viscous it is.

Crude oil is separated into fractions by **fractional/decimal** distillation. Each fraction contains **molecules/ions** with a similar number of carbon atoms. Some fractions are used as fuels. Other fractions are **electrolysed/processed** to make solvents, lubricants, polymers, and detergents.

C Draw lines to match each crude oil fraction to **one** use.

Fraction
gasoline / petrol
diesel oil / gas oil
kerosene
residue
refinery / liquefied petroleum gases (LPG)

Use
aircraft fuels
fuel for car engines
making roads and flat roofs
fuel for heating, camping stoves, and some vehicles
fuel for diesel engines in cars, lorries, and trains and fuel for boilers

D Write the number of each label in a different box on the diagram.

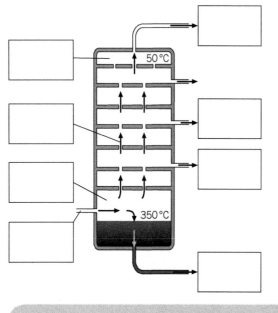

50 °C

350 °C

Labels

1 Vaporised crude oil enters here.

2 coolest part of fractionating column

3 Hydrocarbons with the lowest boiling points leave here, as gases.

4 hottest part of fractionating column

5 Kerosene leaves here.

6 Diesel leaves here.

7 Hydrocarbons with highest boiling points leave the column here, as a thick liquid.

8 Hydrocarbons move up the column. They condense when they reach the temperature of their boiling point.

What you need to remember

Crude oil is separated into _____ using fractional _____ . The properties of a fraction depend on the _____ of its hydrocarbon _____ . Fractions with smaller molecules burn _____ easily than fractions with bigger _____ .

C9.3 Burning hydrocarbon fuels

A Draw lines to make **eight** correct sentences. You do not need all the sentence endings – use only those that make correct sentences.

Sentence starters

| The complete combustion of a hydrocarbon makes |

| Burning methane in a gas cooker |

| Burning diesel in a car |

| A hydrocarbon is only useful as a fuel if |

| When a hydrocarbon burns |

Sentence endings

| carbon dioxide and water. |

| its flammability is low enough. |

| transfers energy to the surroundings. |

| its carbon and hydrogen are oxidised. |

| transfers energy from the surroundings to the hydrocarbon. |

| its flammability is high enough. |

| its carbon and hydrogen are reduced. |

B Balance the equations below for the complete combustion of hydrocarbons.

a $C_3H_8 + \underline{}O_2 \rightarrow \underline{}CO_2 + 4H_2O$

b $CH_4 + \underline{}O_2 \rightarrow CO_2 + \underline{}H_2O$

c $C_5H_{12} + \underline{}O_2 \rightarrow 5CO_2 + \underline{}H_2O$

d $2C_2H_6 + \underline{}O_2 \rightarrow \underline{}CO_2 + \underline{}H_2O$

What you need to remember

When hydrocarbons burn in plenty of air, energy is transferred _____ the surroundings. The carbon and hydrogen are completely _____ to form carbon dioxide and _____ . Hydrocarbons are used as _____ . The incomplete _____ of a hydrocarbon produces toxic carbon _____ , as well as water.

C9.4 Cracking hydrocarbons

A **Cracking** breaks down big hydrocarbon molecules to make hydrocarbons with smaller molecules.

Tick the statements about cracking that are true.

Statement	✓ if true
The products of cracking are less useful than the starting materials.	
The first step of cracking is to vaporise a heavy fraction from the distillation of crude oil.	
One method of cracking involves passing vapours from a heavy fraction of crude oil over a cold catalyst.	
One method of cracking involves mixing steam with vapour from a heavy fraction of crude oil and heating to a high temperature.	

Write corrected versions of the **two** statements that are false.

_____

_____

B Alkenes are a type of hydrocarbon. They are more reactive than alkanes.
You can use bromine water to test for alkenes. In the diagram below:

● Use a crayon to show the colour of bromine water before an alkene is bubbled through it.

● Label the second test tube to show the colour of bromine water after the alkene is bubbled through it.

bromine water
before an alkene is
bubbled through it

bromine water after
an alkene is bubbled
through it

C The equations below show cracking reactions.

● If necessary, balance the symbol equations.

● Circle in red the names of alkenes that are made in cracking. These are used to make polymers.

● Circle in blue the names of alkanes that are made in cracking. These are used in petrol.

a decane → pentane + propene + ethene

$C_{10}H_{22}$ → C_5H_{12} + C_3H_6 + C_2H_4

b dodecane → hexane + propene

$C_{12}H_{26}$ → C_6H_{14} + C_3H_6

What you need to remember

In cracking, large _____ molecules are broken up into smaller ones by passing the vapours over

a hot _____, or by mixing with _____ and heating to a very _____

temperature. Cracking produces shorter-chain _____, which are used as fuels, and alkenes, used to

make _____. Alkenes react with orange _____ water, turning it _____.

C9 Practice questions

01 What is the name of the alkane with the formula C_2H_6?
Tick **one** box. [1 mark]

methane ☐ propane ☐
ethane ☐ butane ☐

02 Which alkane does the structural formula in **Figure 1** represent?

```
    H   H   H
    |   |   |
H — C — C — C — H
    |   |   |
    H   H   H
```

Figure 1
Tick **one** box. [1 mark]

methane ☐ propane ☐
ethane ☐ butane ☐

HINT Start by counting the number of carbon atoms shown in the structural formula.

03 The fractions in crude oil are separated by fractional distillation.

03.1 Heptane is one of the compounds in the petrol fraction. Its formula is C_7H_{16}.
Balance the equation below, which shows the combustion reaction of heptane.
Write **one** number on each line. [3 marks]

$$C_7H_{16} + \_\_O_2 \rightarrow \_\_CO_2 + \_\_H_2O$$

HINT Start by balancing the carbon atoms. There must be the same number of carbon atoms on each side of the arrow.

03.2 A university student measured the boiling point of heptane and octane, which are both substances obtained from crude oil. He measured each boiling point four times.
The student's results are in **Table 1**.

Table 1

Substance	Boiling point in °C			
	Trial 1	Trial 2	Trial 3	Trial 4
heptane	100	98	96	77
octane	125	123	127	125

Write down the name of the hydrocarbon whose set of results includes an anomalous result. [1 mark]

_____

03.3 Calculate the mean boiling point of octane. Give your answer to 3 significant figures. [2 marks]

Mean boiling point = _____ °C

04 The diagram in **Figure 2** shows the apparatus used to crack a hydrocarbon in the laboratory.

Figure 2

04.1 What happens in the boiling tube?
Tick **one** box. [1 mark]

Hydrocarbons are oxidised. ☐
Hydrocarbons are reduced. ☐
Hydrocarbons break down. ☐
Hydrocarbons burn. ☐

04.2 The aluminium oxide shown in **Figure 2** is not used up.
Explain its purpose. [2 marks]

_____

_____

_____

04.3 One of the products produced in the cracking reaction is ethene. Ethene is an alkene.
Describe a chemical test for alkenes. Include the name of the substance you need, brief instructions for doing the test, and the changes you would expect to see. [3 marks]

_____

_____

_____

_____

_____

HINT When you have written your answer, check that you have included everything that the question asks for.

C9 Checklist

	Student Book	☺	😐	☹
I can write down what crude oil is made up of.	9.1			
I can describe what alkanes are.	9.1			
I can represent an alkane by its chemical formula and displayed formula.	9.1			
I can write down the names and formulae of the first four alkanes.	9.1			
I can describe how the volatility, viscosity, and flammability of hydrocarbons are affected by the size of their molecules.	9.2			
I can describe how to separate crude oil into fractions.	9.2			
I can explain the separation of crude oil by fractional distillation.	9.2			
I can describe how the fractions of crude oil are used.	9.2			
I can write down the products formed when you burn hydrocarbons in a good supply of air.	9.3			
I can describe how to test for the products of complete combustion of a hydrocarbon.	9.3			
I can explain why carbon monoxide gas is also made when incomplete combustion takes place.	9.3			
I can write a balanced equation for the complete combustion of a hydrocarbon, given its formula.	9.3			
I can describe how larger, less useful hydrocarbon molecules are cracked to form hydrocarbons with smaller molecules.	9.4			
I can explain why larger, less useful hydrocarbon molecules are cracked to form hydrocarbons with smaller molecules.	9.4			
I can write down examples to illustrate how cracking is useful and how modern life depends on the uses of hydrocarbons.	9.4			
I can describe what alkenes are and how they differ from alkanes.	9.4			

C10.1 Pure substances and mixtures

A In chemistry, what is a pure substance?

Tick the best definition.

O a natural substance that has had nothing added to it ☐

P a natural substance that has not been processed ☐

Q a single element, not mixed with any other substance ☐

R a single element or compound, not mixed with any other substance ☐

B A student melted a yellow solid. The solid started to melt at 32 °C. By 36 °C it had all melted. Which **one** statement about the yellow solid is true?

Tick the true statement.

S It is a pure substance. ☐

T Its melting point is 36 °C. ☐

U It is a mixture of substances. ☐

V Its melting point is 32 °C. ☐

C A student melted four substances. She collected her data in the table. Which substance is pure?

Circle the letter of the pure substance.

Substance	Temperature when it started melting in °C	Temperature when it had all melted in °C
W	22	23
X	97	98
Y	57	60
Z	0	0

D Circle the correct **bold** words in the sentences below.

A formulation is a **compound/mixture** that has been designed as a useful product. Many of the things we use are **simple/complex** mixtures. In a formulation, every element or **compound/mixture** has its own purpose. A formulation is made by **joining together/mixing** its components in the correct quantities to make sure that it has the required properties.

E Circle the formulations in the list below.

petrol   **deodorant**   **paint**   **hair shampoo**   **medicines**

alloys   **seawater**   **fertilisers**   **tinned soup**   **milk**

What you need to remember

Pure substances can be _____ or elements, and they contain only _____ substance. An impure substance is a _____ of two or more _____ or compounds. Pure elements and compounds melt and _____ at specific _____. Mixtures melt and boil over a _____ of temperatures. Formulations are mixtures, made up in carefully _____ quantities so that the product has the required _____.

C10.2 Analysing chromatograms

A Tick next to each correct use of paper chromatography listed below.

Use	✓ if chromatography can be used for this purpose
to show whether a something is a pure substance or a mixture	
to separate mixtures	
to measure boiling points	
to identify substances	
to measure melting points	

B Draw a line to identify the two phases in paper chromatography.

Phase

stationary

mobile

In paper chromatography, this phase is the...

paper

solvent, for example water

C On the chromatogram:

● Circle in pen the substance that has the strongest attraction to the solvent.

● Circle in pencil the substance that has the strongest attraction to the paper.

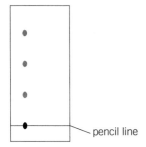

pencil line

D You can use measurements from a chromatogram to calculate the **retention factor (R_f) value** for a substance.

Write the letters below in the correct order to describe how to do this for a food colouring.

Correct order: _____

L Measure the distance that each spot and the solvent front has travelled from the pencil line.

M Use a pencil and ruler to draw a line about 1 cm from the bottom of a strip of chromatography paper.

N Place the paper in a small beaker which contains water to a height of 0.5 cm.

O Dip a capillary tube into the food colouring.

P Calculate the R_f value for each spot using the equation:

$$R_f = \frac{\text{distance moved by substance}}{\text{distance moved by solvent}}$$

Q Briefly touch the end of the capillary tube onto the pencil line so that a spot of food colouring appears on the paper.

R Wait while the water travels up the paper, to a height 0.5 cm below the top of the paper.

What you need to remember

You can use paper chromatography to separate a _____. You can calculate R_f values and match

these to databases to _____ specific substances.

$$\underline{\hspace{3cm}} = \frac{\text{distance moved by substance}}{\text{distance moved by solvent}}$$

C10.3 Testing for gases

A Draw a line to match each gas to its test.

Gas		Test
hydrogen		Limewater turns milky (cloudy).
oxygen		A lighted splint pops.
carbon dioxide		Damp litmus paper is bleached and turns white.
chlorine		A glowing splint relights.

B Which statement best explains why there is a 'pop' sound when you hold a lighted splint at the open end of a test tube of hydrogen gas?

Tick **one** answer.

S The hydrogen reacts explosively with oxygen from the air. ☐

T The hydrogen reacts explosively with nitrogen from the air. ☐

U The wooden splint reacts explosively with oxygen from the air. ☐

V The wooden splint reacts explosively with nitrogen from the air. ☐

C Chlorine is toxic. Which of the safety precautions below should you take **because of its toxicity**?

Circle the correct letter to show your answer.

W Work in a fume cupboard.

X Wear eye protection.

Y Turn off Bunsen burners.

Z Tie back long hair.

D Complete the word equations. Then write down how to test for the gas produced in each reaction.

a magnesium + hydrochloric acid → magnesium chloride + _____

How to test for the gas: _____

Expected result of gas test: _____

b zinc carbonate + sulfuric acid → zinc sulfate + water + _____

How to test for the gas: _____

Expected results of gas test: _____

c hydrogen peroxide → water + _____

How to test for the gas: _____

Expected results of gas test: _____

What you need to remember

When you place a _____ splint in hydrogen gas, the gas burns rapidly with a _____ sound. A glowing splint _____ when you place it in a test tube of _____ gas. Limewater (calcium hydroxide solution) goes _____ when you bubble _____ _____ through it. Chlorine gas _____ damp litmus paper so that the paper goes _____ .

C10 Practice questions

01 What is the test for oxygen gas?
Tick **one** box. [1 mark]

A lighted splint goes out with a pop. ☐

A glowing splint relights. ☐

It makes limewater milky ☐

It bleaches litmus paper. ☐

02 Vitamin and mineral tablets are formulations.

02.1 Define the term *formulation*. [1 mark]

_____

02.2 **Table 1** shows the masses of some of the substances in one type of vitamin and mineral tablet.

Table 1

Substance	Mass in mg
copper sulfate	2
iron fumarate	50
vitamin B6	5
zinc sulfate	25

Which of the substances in **Table 1** is present in the tablet in the greatest amount? [1 mark]

_____

02.3 Calculate the percentage by mass of zinc sulfate in one tablet.
The mass of one tablet is 500 mg. [2 marks]

Answer = _____%

02.4 The formula of iron fumarate is $FeC_4H_2O_4$.
Calculate the relative formula mass of iron fumarate. Use these values of relative atomic mass:
Fe = 56; C = 12; H = 1; O = 16 [2 marks]

Answer = _____

HINT Start by multiplying each relative atomic mass by the number of atoms of this element shown in the formula.

03 A student uses chromatography to analyse a sample of liquid extracted from a nettle leaf.

03.1 Some of the steps of the student's experiment are described below. The student uses a solvent called propanone. The solvent is volatile, meaning it evaporates easily. Give a reason for each stage.

Step 1 Dissolve the sample in the solvent. [1 mark]

Reason: _____

_____

Step 2 Use a pencil (not pen) to draw a line near the bottom of the chromatography paper. [1 mark]

Reason: _____

_____

Step 3 Cover the beaker with a lid. [1 mark]

Reason: _____

_____

Step 4 Mark the final solvent front on the chromatogram. [1 mark]

Reason: _____

_____

03.2 **Figure 1** shows the student's chromatogram. It shows the colours of the pigments in the liquid obtained from the nettle leaf.

Figure 1

Which colour pigment is most soluble in the solvent? Give a reason for your answer. [2 marks]

Pigment: _____

Reason: _____

_____

03.3 Calculate the R_f value for the spot marked **X**.
Give your answer to 2 significant figures.
[3 marks]

R_f value = _____

HINT Use the equation: $R_f = \dfrac{\text{distance moved by spot X from start line}}{\text{distance moved by solvent front from start line}}$

03.4 Which has the greater R_f value, the orange pigment or the green pigment? Explain how you can answer this question without doing a calculation. [2 marks]

_____

_____

_____

_____

C10 Checklist

	Student Book	☺	☺	☹
I can use melting point data to distinguish pure substances from impure substances.	10.1			
I can identify examples of useful mixtures called formulations, given appropriate information.	10.1			
I can describe how chromatography can be used to distinguish pure substances from impure substances.	10.2			
I can explain how chromatography separates mixtures.	10.2			
I can interpret chromatograms.	10.2			
I can use chromatograms to calculate R_f values.	10.2			
I can test for these gases: hydrogen, oxygen, carbon dioxide, and chlorine.	10.3			
I can write down the positive results of tests for hydrogen, oxygen, carbon dioxide, and chlorine.	10.3			

A Why is there little evidence about how the Earth's atmosphere developed?

Tick the best answer.

P The timescale is 4.6 billion years.

Q Algae and plants produced oxygen.

R Volcanoes produced water vapour that condensed.

S Carbon dioxide dissolved in the oceans.

B Draw a line to match each event to when scientists think it happened.

Event	When it happened
planet Earth formed	2.7 billion years ago
intense volcanic activity	4.6 billion years ago
algae first produced oxygen	4.6–3.6 billion years ago

C The flow diagram below summarises one theory about how the Earth's atmosphere was formed and how it developed over time.

Fill in the gaps to complete the diagram.

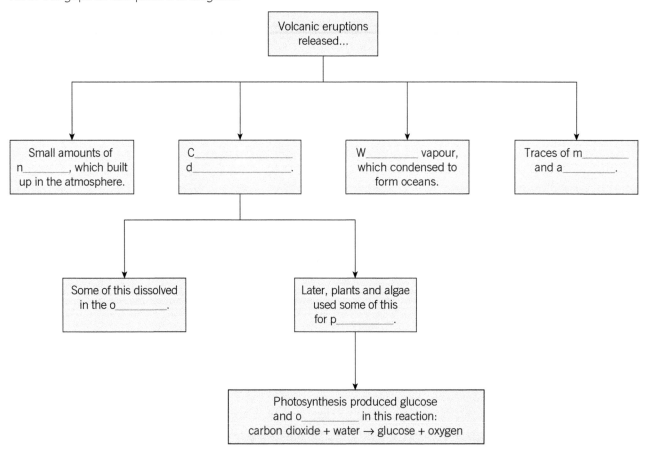

Volcanic eruptions released...

Small amounts of n_____, which built up in the atmosphere.

C_____ d_____.

W_____ vapour, which condensed to form oceans.

Traces of m_____ and a_____.

Some of this dissolved in the o_____.

Later, plants and algae used some of this for p_____.

Photosynthesis produced glucose and o_____ in this reaction:
carbon dioxide + water → glucose + oxygen

What you need to remember

According to one theory, the Earth's early atmosphere was formed by _____ activity. The first atmosphere was mainly _____ . There may also have been _____ vapour, and small amounts of methane and _____ . Algae and _____ produced oxygen by _____ , and over time the amount of oxygen in the atmosphere _____ .

C11.2 Our evolving atmosphere

A The steps below describe one way in which carbon dioxide was removed from the atmosphere, and how its elements ended up in limestone.

Write the letters of the steps in the correct order.

Correct order: _____

T The pressure helped to form rocks such as limestone, which is mainly calcium carbonate ($CaCO_3$).

U Plants and algae took in carbon dioxide (CO_2).

V Animals ate plants, and carbon from the plants ended up in animal tissues, including skeletons and shells.

W Layers of sediment covered the skeletons and shells.

X Plants and algae used carbon dioxide and water to make glucose ($C_6H_{12}O_6$) and oxygen during photosynthesis.

Y The elements of glucose ended up in plant tissue.

Z Over millions of years, skeletons and shells of sea animals built up on the seabed.

B Carbon dioxide was also removed from the atmosphere by the formation of fossil fuels.

Circle the correct **bold** words in the sentences below.

Some ancient plant and **animal/rock** remains were crushed in huge Earth movements, and **cooled/heated** in the Earth's crust. They formed fossil fuels, including **wood/coal**, crude oil, and natural **gas/liquid**.

Coal was formed when **animals/trees** died in swamps. They were buried **with/without** oxygen, and compressed over **millions/hundreds** of years.

Oil and gas formed from **plankton/dinosaur** remains that fell into **rocks/mud** on the seabed. The remains were covered by **sediments/water** that became layers of **rock/mud** over millions of years. Oil and **natural liquid/ natural gas** are found below this rock.

C Draw a line to match each gas to its percentage in the modern atmosphere of the Earth.

Gas	Percentage of the atmosphere
nitrogen	0.9%
oxygen	78%
argon	trace amounts
carbon dioxide	21%
other gases	0.04%

What you need to remember

The amount of carbon dioxide in the early atmosphere decreased because of _____, and the formation of _____ rocks and _____ fuels. Today, 78% of the atmosphere is _____ and 21% is _____. There are smaller amounts of _____, carbon dioxide, and other gases.

C11.3 Greenhouse gases

A Circle the names of the **three** main greenhouse gases in the list below.

water vapour   oxygen   carbon dioxide   methane   nitrogen

B Tick the **one** correct box in each row.

Human activity	✓ if this activity results in more carbon dioxide in the atmosphere	✓ if this activity results in more methane in the atmosphere	✓ if this activity reduces the amount of carbon dioxide absorbed by 'CO$_2$ sinks'
burning fossil fuels			
adding waste to landfill sites			
farming cattle			
growing rice			
cutting down trees			

C Label the diagram by writing the number of **one** label in each box.

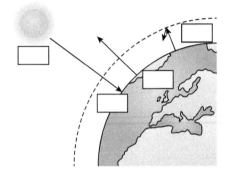

1 Short-wavelength ultraviolet radiation passes through the layer of greenhouse gases.	**2** The Sun emits radiation.	**3** The surface of the Earth cools by emitting longer wavelength infrared radiation.

4 Greenhouse gases absorb infrared radiation, so some energy radiated by the surface of the Earth is trapped here.

D Tick the statements below that are true.

Statement	✓ if true
Most scientists agree that a trend in global warming has started.	
Evidence in scientific journals does not support the existence of global warming.	
Evidence in scientific journals is peer reviewed (checked by other scientists).	
Articles in the media about global warming are always true.	

Write corrected versions of the **two** statements that are false.

_____

_____

What you need to remember

Greenhouse gases in the atmosphere maintain temperatures on Earth _____ enough to support life.

Human activities _____ the amount of greenhouse gases, including _____

_____ and _____, in the atmosphere. Most peer-reviewed _____ agrees

that increased amounts of greenhouse gases will _____ average global temperatures.

C11.4 Global climate change

A An increase in average global temperature is a major cause of climate change.

Draw lines to make **six** correct sentences about climate change.

Sentence starters

Rising sea levels happen because of

Climate change includes more frequent extreme weather events

Changes in temperature and rainfall patterns

Sentence endings

might result in certain crops growing less well in some areas.

ice caps melting.

might result in certain crops growing better in some areas.

such as more severe storms.

water expanding at higher temperatures.

might result in the extinctions of some species.

B Fill in the gaps to complete the definition of **carbon footprint.**

The carbon footprint of a product, service, or event is the total amount of _____ _____ and other _____ gases emitted over its full life cycle.

C Write the number of each phrase below the table in the correct column of the table.

Ways of reducing the amount of carbon dioxide humans put into the atmosphere	Ways of reducing the amount of methane humans put into the atmosphere

1 Generate electricity from renewable resources, not fossil fuels.	2 Use cars less.	3 Reduce the demand for beef and dairy products.
4 Develop carbon capture technologies to store carbon dioxide in porous rocks underground.	5 Insulate homes.	6 Reduce waste sent to landfill.

What you need to remember

Increasing greenhouse _____ cause higher average global _____, leading to _____ change. We can reduce greenhouse gas emissions by _____ the use of fossil _____ .

C11.5 Atmospheric pollutants

A The air pollutants below are formed when fossil fuels burn.

Draw lines to match each pollutant to its chemical formula and one or more of its effects.

Pollutant	Formula	Effects of pollutant
sulfur dioxide	CO	acid rain
nitrogen oxides	NO and NO_2	breathing problems
carbon monoxide	SO_2	toxic gas that can kill
soot (carbon particles, or particulates)	C	global dimming
		damages lung cells and may cause cancer

B Circle the correct **bold** words in the sentences below and complete the word equations to explain how air pollutants form.

Fossil fuels contain carbon and **helium/hydrogen**. The combustion, or burning, of a fossil fuel in plenty of air makes carbon dioxide and **oxygen/water**. For example:

methane + _____ → carbon dioxide + water

Some fuels, including coal, contain some sulfur. When the fuel burns, sulfur **carbonate/dioxide** is formed:

sulfur + oxygen → sulfur _____

High temperatures in car engines mean that nitrogen and **argon/oxygen** from the air can react together. The reactions make nitrogen oxides. For example:

nitrogen + _____ → _____ dioxide

When there is **too much/not enough** oxygen in an engine, incomplete combustion of hydrocarbons occurs. This means that carbon **monoxide/trioxide** forms as well as carbon dioxide. For example:

hexane + _____ → carbon dioxide + carbon _____ + water

Some of the big hydrocarbon molecules in **diesel/methane** do not burn completely. They make **huge/tiny** pieces of solid containing carbon and **burnt/unburnt** hydrocarbons. These are particulates.

What you need to remember

Burning fossil fuels makes carbon dioxide and _____ . When a fossil fuel burns in a poor supply of oxygen, poisonous carbon _____ also forms. In diesel engines, particulates (_____ and unburned hydrocarbons) are formed. These cause lung damage and global _____ . Sulfur impurities in fuels burn to make _____ _____ . At the _____ temperature of a car engine, _____ and oxygen react to make nitrogen oxides. Sulfur dioxide and nitrogen oxides cause _____ problems and _____ rain.

C11 Practice questions

01 Draw **one** line from each gas to a problem it causes. [3 marks]

Gas	Problem it causes
carbon monoxide	global dimming
particulates	toxic to humans
oxides of nitrogen	climate change
carbon dioxide	acid rain

02 Oxides of nitrogen are formed when nitrogen and oxygen from the air react together at the high temperatures of car engines.

02.1 Write a balanced symbol equation to show the reaction of nitrogen and oxygen to form nitrogen monoxide. [3 marks]

_____

HINT Use these formulae: N_2 O_2 NO

02.2 **Table 1** shows the concentrations of oxides of nitrogen in the air in seven areas of the UK. The values given are mean values, calculated over one whole year.

Table 1

Area	Mean concentration of oxides of nitrogen in the air in 2011 in $\mu g/m^3$
Bristol	56
Hull	67
London	136
Manchester	74
Portsmouth	64
Scottish Borders	27
South Wales	70

Plot the data from **Table 1** on a bar chart on **Figure 1**. [2 marks]

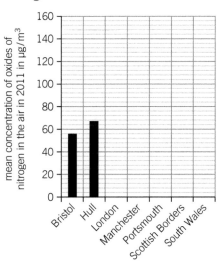

Figure 1

02.3 Describe the difference in values between Bristol and London, and suggest **two** reasons for this difference. [4 marks]

_____

_____

_____

02.4 **Table 1** gives concentration values in micrograms per cubic metre ($\mu g/m^3$).
Calculate the concentration in London in grams per cubic metre (g/m^3). [2 marks]

Answer = _____ g/m^3

HINT Start by completing this equation:
1 microgram (μg) = _____ g.

02.5 In the month of August, a university student collected five readings for the concentration of oxides of nitrogen in the air in Hull. **Table 2** shows her results.

Table 2

Place	Concentration of oxides of nitrogen in $\mu g/m^3$				
	Value 1	Value 2	Value 3	Value 4	Value 5
Hull	50	55	51	55	52

Calculate the mean concentration of oxides of nitrogen in Hull in August from the values in **Table 2**. Give your answer to 2 significant figures. [1 mark]

Mean concentration of oxides of nitrogen =

_____ $\mu g/m^3$

02.6 Suggest why the mean you calculated for Hull using data from **Table 2** is different from the value for Hull given in **Table 1**. [1 mark]

_____

_____

HINT Look at the time periods over which the data were collected.

02.7 Give **two** reasons why the government wants to reduce the concentration of oxides of nitrogen in the air, and suggest how the government could achieve this aim. [6 marks]

_____

_____

_____

C11 Checklist

	Student Book	☺	☹	☹
I can describe a theory about how our atmosphere developed.	11.1			
I can interpret evidence and evaluate different theories about the Earth's early atmosphere, given appropriate information.	11.1			
I can describe the main changes in the atmosphere over time, and explain likely causes of these changes.	11.2			
I can write down the relative proportions of gases in our atmosphere.	11.2			
I can explain how the greenhouse effect operates.	11.3			
I can evaluate the quality of evidence in a report about global climate change, given appropriate information.	11.3			
I can describe uncertainties in the evidence for global warming.	11.3			
I can explain the importance of peer review of results and of communicating results to a wide range of audiences.	11.3			
I can describe how emissions of carbon dioxide and methane can be reduced.	11.4			
I can explain why actions to reduce greenhouse gas emissions may be limited.	11.4			
I can explain the scale, risk, and environmental implications of global climate change.	11.4			
I can write down the products of combustion of a fuel, given the composition of the fuel and the conditions in which it is used.	11.5			
I can describe the problems caused by increased amounts of pollutants in the air.	11.5			

C12.1 Finite and renewable resources

A Some resources are finite, and others are renewable.

Tick the **one** correct box in each row.

Resource	✓ if the resource is finite	✓ if the resource is renewable
crude oil		
crops used to make biofuels		
coal		
softwoods		

B Many natural materials have been replaced by synthetic materials.

Write each term below in the correct box of the table.

cling film   **clothes**   **ropes**

acrylic   **wool**   **window frames**

Natural resource	Use	Synthetic material
wood		PVC
sisal		poly(propene)
cotton	covering food	

C Reserves of copper are ore deposits that have been discovered and would be profitable to mine. The bar chart shows the estimated reserves of copper in the Earth's crust in different years.

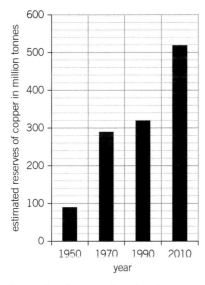

a Describe the trend in the data. _____

b The actual amount of copper in the Earth's crust has not changed. Suggest why the estimated reserves have changed.

_____

c Suggest why we cannot be certain about the copper reserve at any time.

_____

What you need to remember

We use the Earth's natural _____ to make products and for fuels. Some resources are finite and

others are _____ . Estimates of when particular _____ resources will run out vary

because there are many _____ in the calculations.

C12.2 Water safe to drink

A Circle the correct **bold** words in the sentences below.

Potable water is water that is **safe/unsafe** to drink. It **is/is not** pure, because it contains dissolved substances. Potable water has **low/high** levels of dissolved salts and **low/high** levels of microbes.

In the UK, **rainwater/seawater** collects in the ground and in rivers and lakes. It is also stored in reservoirs.

B The flow chart shows how water is made safe to drink in the UK.

Fill in the gaps to complete the flow chart.

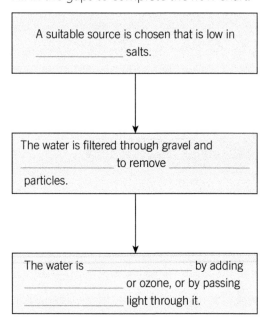

A suitable source is chosen that is low in _____ salts.

The water is filtered through gravel and _____ to remove _____ particles.

The water is _____ by adding _____ or ozone, or by passing _____ light through it.

C Tick to show which statements are true.

Statement	✓ if true
In countries with wet climates and plenty of natural sources of fresh water, potable water can be obtained from seawater.	
Most potable water that is obtained from seawater is obtained by distillation.	
Distillation is one method of desalination.	
The energy costs of the distillation of seawater are low.	
A process called reverse osmosis uses membranes to remove dissolved salts from water.	
Reverse osmosis involves heating, so it requires more energy than distillation.	

Write corrected versions of the **three** statements that are false.

_____

_____

_____

What you need to remember

In the UK, potable water is obtained by choosing a suitable water _____, filtering the water, and _____ it with chlorine, ozone, or _____ light. In _____ countries, potable water can be obtained from seawater by _____ and _____ osmosis. Both these processes have _____ energy requirements.

C12.3 Treating waste water

A Waste water must be treated before it is released to the environment.

Complete the flow diagram by writing one of the phrases below it in each box.

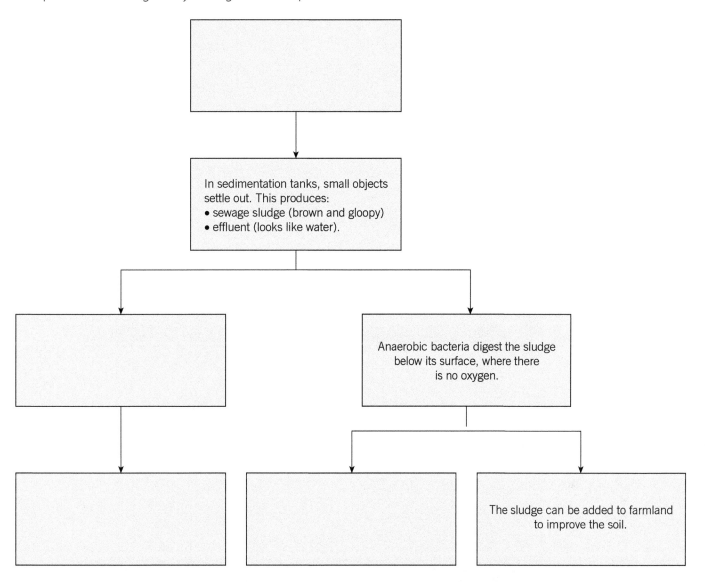

Phrases

- The sludge can be used as a source of renewable energy.
- Air bubbles through the effluent. Aerobic bacteria break down harmful microorganisms.
- The effluent flows into a river.
- Screening removes big, solid objects and then grit.

What you need to remember

Sewage treatment starts with removing _____ objects and grit. In the first tank, a process called _____ produces _____ and effluent. The effluent is treated by _____ bacteria. The sludge is digested by _____ bacteria. In general, it is easier to obtain drinking _____ from ground water than from waste water or seawater.

C12.5 Life Cycle Assessments

A Use the words below to fill in the gaps.

packaging   sources   environment   reusing

raw materials   wastes   disposing   water

A Life Cycle Assessment (LCA) assesses the impact on the _____ of a product. An LCA has four stages:

- getting and processing the _____
- making the product and its _____
- using and _____ the product
- _____ of the product.

An LCA takes into account the uses of _____, raw materials, and energy _____. It also takes into account the _____ produced.

B An LCA is carried out on manufactured products.

Write the inputs and outputs of an LCA below in the correct columns of the table.

raw materials   energy   water   solid waste   emissions to the atmosphere

other products made alongside the product   waste that goes into rivers and the sea

Inputs	Outputs

C Tick to show which aspects of an LCA can easily be given a numerical value.

Aspect of LCA	✓ if it can be given a numerical value	✓ if it cannot easily be given a numerical value
raw materials needed		
water required in manufacture		
impact of noise during manufacture		
fuel used in distribution		
impact on pedestrians of distribution vehicles		
waste gases		
impact of waste gases on human health		
impact on wildlife of waste that enters rivers		

What you need to remember

Life Cycle Assessments assess the _____ impacts of _____, processes, or services. An LCA analyses each stage of the _____ _____, including getting the _____ materials, making and _____ the product, and disposing of the product. It is not _____ to give numerical values for the effects of pollutants, so many LCAs include judgements that are a matter of _____.

C12.6 Reduce, reuse, and recycle

A Choose words from the list to complete the sentences below.

recycled   **quarrying**   **reuse**   **recycling**   **materials**

a Metals, glass, plastics, and building materials are made from limited raw _____.

b Obtaining raw materials from the Earth by mining and _____ causes environmental impacts.

c You can use a glass bottle again. This is called _____.

d The process by which waste objects are processed so that their materials are used again is called _____.

e Many products that cannot be reused can be _____.

B Tick the correct column to indicate whether each action is an example of reuse or recycling.

Action	✓ if the action is an example of reuse	✓ if the action is an example of recycling
Crushing glass bottles, melting them, and making new bottles.		
Giving your coat to your little sister or brother when it is too small for you.		
Collecting gold from used mobile phones, melting the gold, and making rings from it.		
Giving your old mobile phone to a charity that makes sure it works before giving it to someone who cannot afford to buy their own.		

C The flow diagram below shows how aluminium is recycled. Fill in the gaps to complete the flow diagram.

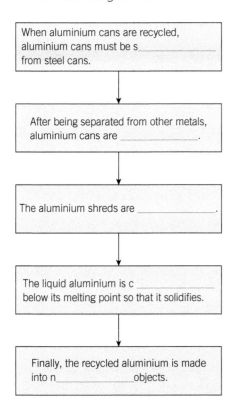

When aluminium cans are recycled, aluminium cans must be s_____ from steel cans.

↓

After being separated from other metals, aluminium cans are _____.

↓

The aluminium shreds are _____.

↓

The liquid aluminium is c_____ below its melting point so that it solidifies.

↓

Finally, the recycled aluminium is made into n_____ objects.

What you need to remember

The Earth has limited supplies of raw materials, such as _____ ores. There are social, economic, and _____ issues linked with using these resources. Recycling metals saves _____, finite metal ores, and fossil _____. Recycling also _____ the pollution caused by the mining and extraction of metals.

C12 Practice questions

01 This question is about the Life Cycle Assessment (LCA) of a smart phone.

01.1 Draw **one** line from each activity to a stage in the life cycle of a smart phone.
Each stage in the life cycle may be linked to one or more activities. [4 marks]

Activity	Stage in life cycle
extracting oil from oil wells under the sea to make plastic	obtaining and processing raw materials
messaging friends	
giving the phone to a younger brother or sister when it is no longer fashionable	making the product and packaging
extracting metals from their ores to make circuit components	using the product
putting together the components in a plastic or metal case	
recycling phone components	disposing of the product and packaging

01.2 A mobile phone company take three different actions to reduce the environmental impact of its phones. For each action below:

- identify which stage in the life cycle the action will affect
- explain how the action will reduce the environmental impact of the phone.

Action 1 Reducing the electric current needed to operate the phone.
Stage in life cycle: _____

How the action will reduce the environmental impact of the phone:

_____

_____ [2 marks]

Action 2 Making the phone case from grass mixed with a resin, instead of plastic or metal.
Stage in life cycle: _____
How the action will reduce the environmental impact of the phone:

_____

_____ [2 marks]

Action 3 Making the phone from separate modules that can be replaced when they break.
Stage in life cycle: _____
How the action will reduce the environmental impact of the phone:

_____

_____ [2 marks]

02 This question is about bottled water.

02.1 **Table 1** shows the concentrations of some ions in a bottle of water.

Table 1

Formula of ion	Concentration in mg/litre
Ca^{2+}	61
Na^+	11
Mg^{2+}	7
K^+	1
NO_3^-	18
SO_4^{2-}	14

Name the ion with the formula SO_4^{2-}. [1 mark]

_____

02.2 A person drinks 0.5 litres of water.
Calculate the mass of calcium she has consumed. [2 marks]

Mass of calcium = _____ mg

HINT The table shows the mass dissolved in one whole litre of water.

02.3 A typical adult needs 300 mg of magnesium a day.
Calculate the volume of water an adult would need to drink to consume this mass of magnesium.
Give your answer to 2 significant figures. [3 marks]

Volume of water = _____ litres

HINT Look at the table to find the mass of magnesium in 1 litre of water. Then work out how many litres of water would contain 300 mg of magnesium.

02.4 Use your answer to **02.3** to suggest why it is important to consume other sources of magnesium in addition to water. [1 mark]

_____

_____

C12 Checklist

	Student Book	☺	😐	☹
I can write down examples of natural products that are supplemented or replaced by agricultural or synthetic products.	12.1			
I can distinguish between finite and renewable resources, given appropriate information.	12.1			
I can extract and interpret information about resources from charts, graphs, and tables.	12.1			
I can use orders of magnitude to evaluate the significance of data.	12.1			
I can explain the difference between potable water and pure water.	12.2			
I can describe the differences in treatment of ground water and salty water.	12.2			
I can describe how to do a simple distillation of salt solution and test the distillate to determine its purity.	12.2			
I can describe how waste water is made safe to release into the environment.	12.3			
I can compare how easy it is to obtain potable water from waste water, ground water, and salty water.	12.3			
I can describe how to carry out simple comparative Life Cycle Assessments for shopping bags made from plastic and paper.	12.5			
I can interpret Life Cycle Assessments of materials and products, given appropriate information.	12.5			
I can explain how using less, reusing, and recycling of materials decreases their environmental impact.	12.5			
I can evaluate ways of reducing the use of limited supplies of metal ores, given appropriate information.	12.5			

Answers

C1.1

A atoms – the tiny particle that makes up all substances
element – a substance containing only one type of atom
compound – a substance containing atoms of more than one element, strongly joined together

B from top: electron, nucleus

C chlorine – Cl
hydrogen – H
oxygen – O
sodium – Na
sulfur – S

D O_2 – *element*
Cl_2 – *element*
H_2O – *compound*
H_2 – *element*
CO_2 – *compound*

E non-metals, 6, metals, 2, 1

What you need to remember
atoms, nucleus, electrons, elements, compounds, periodic table, groups, chemical properties, left, non-metals

C1.2

A The starting substances are called products – *false*
The substances that are made are called products – *true*
The number of atoms of each element does not change – *true*
The total mass of products is greater than the total mass of reactants – *false*
The atoms rearrange themselves and join together differently – *true*

Corrected versions:
The starting substances are called reactants.
The total mass of products is equal to the total mass of reactants.

B a carbon + **oxygen** → carbon dioxide
    b copper carbonate →
            copper oxide + **carbon dioxide**

C a **2**Mg + O_2 → 2MgO
    b **2**H_2 + O_2 → **2**H_2O

D a $CuCO_3$(**s**) → CuO(**s**) + CO_2(**g**)
    b 2Mg(**s**) + O_2(**g**) → 2MgO(**s**)

E a copper carbonate decomposes on heating; one of the products is carbon dioxide gas, which escapes to the air
    b magnesium reacts with oxygen from the air on heating; the product is magnesium oxide gas; the apparent extra mass comes from the oxygen that the magnesium reacts with

What you need to remember
reactants, products, destroyed, products, solid, aqueous solution

C1.3

A Its elements can be separated only in chemical reactions – *compounds only*
It contains more than one element – *mixtures and compounds*
Its elements or compounds can be separated by physical means, such as filtration – *mixtures*
There are chemical bonds between its different elements – *compounds*
The ratio of elements in it is always the same – *compounds*

B **Z, W, X, Y**

C left, from top: steam, salt solution
right, from top: thermometer, water out, condenser, water in, beaker, pure water

D You can separate salt – from seawater – by crystallisation.
You can separate sand – from seawater – by filtration.
You can separate seaweed – from seawater – by filtration.
You can separate water – from seawater – by distillation.

What you need to remember
mixture, filtration, crystallisation, distillation

C1.4

A **Z** green and pink

B Paper chromatography – separates mixtures of compounds dissolved in a solvent – because some compounds dissolve better in the solvent than others.
Fractional distillation – separates mixtures of miscible liquids – with different boiling points.

C a **FD**
    b **C**
    c **FD**

D anticlockwise, from top left: **2, 3** or **4, 3** or **4, 1, 5, 6**

What you need to remember
miscible, boiling, fractionating, chromatography, solvent, dissolve

C1.5

A **proton** – A tiny particle with a positive charge. It is found in the nucleus of an atom.
neutron – A tiny particle with a positive charge. It is found in the nucleus of an atom.
electron – A tiny particle with a negative charge. It is found outside the nucleus of an atom.
nucleus – The small and dense central part of an atom.

B This model includes electrons – *both models*
In this model there is a dense positive charge at the centre of the atom – *nuclear model*
In this model the positive charge is spread all over the atom – *'plum pudding' model*
In this model the positive and negative charges balance out – *both models*

C positively, all, bounced back, evidence, positive, repels

What you need to remember
changed, evidence, models, electrons, positive, nuclear, positive.

C1.6

A proton – +1, **1**
neutron – 0, **1**
electron – –1, $\dfrac{1}{2000}$

B atomic number = number of protons – *always correct*
number of protons = number of neutrons – *not always correct*
mass number = number of protons + number of neutrons – *always correct*
number of neutrons = atomic number – mass number – *not always correct*

Corrected versions:
number of protons = number of electrons
number of neutrons = mass number – atomic number

C lithium – 3, 4, **3, 7**
beryllium – 4, 5, **4, 9**
fluorine – 9, 10, **9, 19**
neon – 10, 10, **10, 20**
gold – 79, 118, **79, 197**

D 15, 15, 16, 13, 13, 27, 14

What you need to remember
neutrons, charge, mass, electron, mass, electrons, protons, neutrons, protons, electrons

C1.7

A carbon – $^{12}_{6}C$, **12, 6**
lithium – $^{7}_{3}Li$, **7, 3**
sulfur – $^{32}_{16}S$, **32, 16**

B The radius of an atom is approximately – 0.000 000 000 1 m, which is the same as – 1×10^{-10} m, which is the same as – 0.1 nanometres – or 0.1 nm.
The radius of a nucleus is approximately – 0.000 000 000 00 001 m, which is the same as – 1×10^{-14} m, which is the same as – 0.000 01 nanometres – or 0.000 01 nm.

C a 2+
    b –18
    c 8, –10
    d 17, 1–

D Isotopes are atoms of the same element with different numbers of neutrons – *true*
Isotopes of an element have the same mass number but different atomic numbers – *false*
Samples of different isotopes of an element have different physical properties – *true*

Samples of different isotopes of an element have different chemical properties – *false*
The symbols show two isotopes of the same element: $^{14}_{6}C$ and $^{12}_{6}C$ – *true*

Corrected versions:
Isotopes of an element have the same atomic number but different mass numbers.
Samples of different isotopes of an element have the same chemical properties.

What you need to remember
mass, atomic, ion, negative, positive, isotopes

C1.8

A energy, lowest, lowest
B 1 (shown nearest the nucleus) – 2
  2 – 8
  3 – 8
C a 2, 7
  b 2, 8, 1
  c 1
D S
E a **NG**
  b **NG**
  c **NG**
  d –
  e –
  f **NG**

What you need to remember
energy, lowest, electrons, eight, properties, outer

C1 Practice questions

01 copper oxide [1]
02 H_2O [1]
03 dyes in felt-tip pens – chromatography
   water from salty water – distillation
   solid copper sulfate from copper sulfate solution – crystallisation
   sand from a mixture of sand and salty water – filtration [3; 2 for 3 correct; 1 for 1 or 2 correct]
04 wear eye protection; [1] place the solution in the evaporating dish; [1] place the tripod on the heatproof mat, and the gauze on the tripod; [1] heat the contents of the evaporating dish with the Bunsen burner; [1] when the volume of the solution is roughly halved, stop heating; [1] when cool, place the evaporating dish and its contents in a warm, dry place to allow crystals to form [1]
05.1 6 [1]
05.2 5 [1]
05.3 23 [1]
05.4 eight crosses drawn on the middle circle and one cross drawn on the outer circle [1]
05.5 2, 8, 1 [1]
05.6 $^{11}_{5}Y$ [1]

C2.1

A The periodic table – classifies elements according to their properties.
  The periodic table – groups together elements with similar properties.
  The periodic table – lists all the elements in order of atomic number.
  Mendeleev – changed the order of some elements to group them with other elements with similar properties.
  Mendeleev – left gaps for elements that he predicted did exist, but which had not yet been discovered.
  Because of isotopes, – some elements ended up in the 'wrong' groups when the elements were put in order of atomic weight.
B a atomic
  b elements
  c order
  d gaps
  e properties
  f discovered
  g patterns

What you need to remember
elements, properties, repeating, elements, periodic

C2.2

A properties that are typical of metals – high melting point, ductile, malleable
  properties that are typical of non-metals – low melting point, brittle
B In the periodic table, the elements are arranged in order of decreasing atomic number from left to right of a period (horizontal row) – *false*
  In the periodic table, elements in the same group have the same number of electrons in their outer shell – *true*
  Elements in the same group of the periodic table have similar chemical reactions – *true*
  Metals react to form positive ions – *true*

  Corrected version:
  In the periodic table, the elements are arranged in order of increasing atomic number from left to right of a period (horizontal row).
C

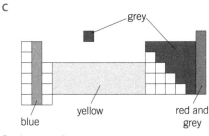

D increases, increases, gas

What you need to remember
group, electrons, chemical, 0, electronic

C2.3

A alkali, similar, outer, reactive, stable, more
B When you expose an alkali metal to air – its surface goes dull – because a layer of oxide forms.
  When you burn an alkali metal in chlorine – it makes a white product, – which is a chloride.
  When you place an alkali metal in water – it fizzes – because hydrogen gas forms.
  When you place sodium in water – it floats – because it is less dense than water.
  When you place an alkali metal in water with universal indicator – the solution becomes purple – because one of the products is alkaline.
C lithium + **oxygen** → lithium oxide
  sodium + chlorine → **sodium chloride**
  potassium + water → potassium hydroxide + **hydrogen**
  sodium + water → **sodium hydroxide** + water
D a $2Na + Cl_2 \rightarrow 2NaCl$
  b $4Li + O_2 \rightarrow 2Li_2O$
  c $2K + 2H_2O \rightarrow 2KOH + H_2$
  d $2Li + Cl_2 \rightarrow 2LiCl$
  e $4Na + O_2 \rightarrow 2Na_2O$
E a there would be an explosive reaction, and observers would see fizzing and flames; the green solution would become purple
  b rubidium + water → rubidium hydroxide + hydrogen

What you need to remember
alkali, electronic, electron, water, oxides, chlorine

C2.4

A a 7
  b 7
  c 1
  d 2
B diagram on right
C increases, increases, increases, decreases
D The elements share electrons in these compounds – *true for compounds of halogens with hydrogen*
  These compounds include ions of halogens, with a single negative charge – *true for compounds of halogens with metals*
  These compounds are white solids – *true for compounds of halogens with metals*
E bromine and potassium chloride solution – no,
  chlorine and sodium iodide solution – yes,
  chlorine + sodium iodide → sodium chloride + iodine

What you need to remember
metals, negative, sharing, non-metals or elements, more, less, increase, decreases

C2.5

A caesium, lithium, iodine, fluorine
B Each atom of an element in this group needs one extra electron to fill its outermost shell – *true for Group 7*

Each atom of an element in this group needs to give away an electron so that its outermost shell is full – *true for Group 1*

When an element in this group forms a compound with a metal, the atoms gain one extra electron – *true for Group 7*

When an element in this group forms a compound with a non-metal, the atoms give away one electron – *true for Group 1*

C   sodium, less, fluorine, more

What you need to remember

more, less, one, one

C2 Practice questions

01.1   N **or** Ne [1]
01.2   Ne [1]
01.3   Mg **and** Sr [1]
01.4   Mg **or** Sr [1]
02   W and Y [1]
03.1   fluorine exists as molecules [1] each made up of two fluorine atoms [1]
03.2   iodine **or** astatine [1]
03.3 $Cl_2(aq) + 2NaBr(aq) \rightarrow 2NaCl(\mathbf{aq}) + Br_2(\mathbf{l})$ [2]
03.4   displacement [1]
03.5   going down the group, [1] melting point increases [1]
03.6   no, because this is lower than the melting point of bromine; the pattern suggests that the melting point of iodine is higher than that of bromine [1]

C3.1

A   Solids – have a fixed shape.
    Solids – cannot be compressed.
    Solids – have a fixed volume.
    Liquids – can flow.
    Liquids – have no fixed shape.
    Liquids – have a fixed volume.
    Gases – can flow.
    Gases – can be compressed easily.
    Gases – have no fixed shape.
B   solid → liquid – melt
    liquid → gas – evaporate/boil
    gas → liquid – condense
    liquid → solid – freeze
    solid → gas – sublime
C   solid – particles arranged in a regular pattern, touching each other
    liquid – particles randomly arranged, touching each other
    gas – particles randomly arranged, far apart from each other
D   When ice is melting, energy is being transferred from the ice to the surroundings – *false*
    When steam is condensing, energy is being transferred to the steam from the surroundings – *true*
    When ice melts, its particles break away from their fixed positions and start moving around – *true*
    When steam condenses, its particles become further apart – *false*

Corrected versions:
    When ice is melting, energy is being transferred from the surroundings to the ice.
    When steam condenses, its particles become closer together.

What you need to know

liquid, particles, vibrate, liquid, move, further, randomly, from, transferred, surroundings

C3.2

A   **ion** – a charged particle made when an atom loses or gains one or more electrons
    covalent bonding – the attraction between atoms that share electrons
    ionic bonding – the attraction between oppositely charged ions
    dot and cross diagram – a diagram showing only the outer shell electrons of the atoms or ions in a substance
B   one electron, loses, an ion, noble gas, gains, chloride, 2.8.8, stable
C   sodium ion – two electrons in first shell, eight electrons in second shell
    chloride ion – two electrons in first shell, eight electrons in second shell, eight electrons in third shell
D   chlorine – 2,8,7, Cl^-, **2,8,8**
    fluorine – 2,7, F^-, **2,8**
    lithium – 2,1, Li^+, **2**
    oxygen – 2,6, O^{2-}, **2,8**
    magnesium – 2,8,2, Mg^{2+}, **2,8**

What you need to remember

gaining, atom, electrons, 7, noble

C3.3

A   Atoms of metals form – positive ions.
    Atoms of non-metals form – negative ions.
    Atoms of Group 1 elements form – ions with a single charge, positive ions.
    Atoms of Group 7 elements form – ions with a single charge, negative ions.
    Ionic bonds form – between oppositely charged ions.
B   oxygen – 6, 2–
    rubidium – 1, 1+
    sulfur – 6, 2–
    iodine – 7, 1–
    magnesium – 2, 2+
    calcium – 2, 2+
C   a   7 crosses and 1 dot around F^-, Li^+ is (2), F^- is (2, 8)
    b   6 crosses and 2 dots around O^{2-}, Ca^{2+} is (2, 8, 8) and O^{2-} is (2, 8)
    c   7 crosses and 1 dot around Cl^-, Mg^{2+} is (2, 8) and Cl^- is (2, 8, 8)

What you need to remember

positive, forces, ionic, 1, 2, 6, 1–

C3.4

A   huge, lattice, strong, ions, all, ionic, high
B   both diagrams: all ions marked + in grey, all ions marked – in green

C   High boiling point – A large amount of energy is needed to break the many strong bonds.
    Conducts electricity as a liquid (when melted) – The ions are free to move.
    Conducts electricity when dissolved in water – The ions are free to move.
D   left box – **T, V, Y**
    middle box – **Z**
    right box – **U, W, X**

What you need to remember

ions, electrostatic, energy, high, high, dissolved, ions

C3.5

A   Atoms of metal elements join together by sharing pairs of electrons – *false*
    Atoms of non-metal elements may get the stable electronic structure of a noble gas by sharing electrons – *true*
    A covalent bond is the bond between two atoms that a pair of electrons – *true*
    One shared pair of electrons is one covalent bond – *true*
    Covalent bonds are weak – *false*
    Corrected versions:
    Atoms of non-metal elements join together by sharing pairs of electrons.
    Covalent bonds are strong.
B   chlorine, hydrogen, hydrogen bromide, nitrogen dioxide, sulfur
C   hydrogen – single
    hydrogen chloride – 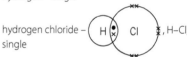 , H–Cl, single

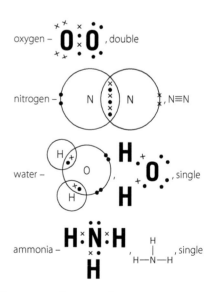

oxygen – double
nitrogen – N≡N
water – single
ammonia – single

What you need to remember

non-metals, single

C3.6

A   low melting points – The forces between molecules (the **intermolecular forces**) are weak, so relatively little energy is needed to overcome them.

do not conduct electricity – The molecules have no overall electrical charge.

low boiling points – The forces between molecules (the **intermolecular forces**) are weak, so relatively little energy is needed to overcome them.

usually exist as gases or liquids at room temperature – The forces between molecules (the **intermolecular forces**) are weak, so relatively little energy is needed to overcome≈them.

B   They are made from many small reactive molecules, joined together to form long chains – *true*

Poly(ethene) is made up from thousands of small ethene molecules, joined together in long chains – *true*

The intermolecular forces between polymer molecules are weaker than the intermolecular forces between smaller molecules – *false*

In general, polymers have lower melting and boiling points than substances made up of smaller molecules – *false*

Many polymers are in the gas state at room temperature – *false*

Corrected versions:

The intermolecular forces between polymer molecules are stronger than the intermolecular forces between smaller molecules.

In general, polymers have higher melting and boiling points than substances made up of smaller molecules.

Many polymers are in the solid state at room temperature.

C   *3D ball and stick model*
advantage: shows how the bonds are orientated in space
disadvantage: Does not show that the atoms are touching each other in the molecule

displayed formula showing bonds
advantage: shows that there is one single bond between each carbon and hydrogen atom.
disadvantage: does not show that the atoms are touching each other in the molecule

dot and cross diagram showing outer shell electrons
advantage: shows that each bond has one electron from a carbon atom and one electron from a hydrogen atom
disadvantage: does not show how the bonds are orientated in space

(These are example answers only – there are many other acceptable responses.)

What you need to remember
weak, low, no, electricity, weaknesses.

C3.7

A   diamond only: **V**
diamond and graphite: **S, T, Z**
graphite only: **U, W, X, Y**

B   It has a high melting point – Each atom is joined by strong covalent bonds to three other atoms. Large amounts of energy are needed to break all these bonds.

It is insoluble in water – Its covalent bonds are very strong, so they do not break when it is placed in water.

It is soft – Its layers slide over each other.

It conducts electricity – There are electrons between its layers which are free to move. Since these particles are negatively charged, they drift away from the negative terminal of a battery.

What you need to remember
giant, graphite, high, diamond, soft, conduct, move, delocalised

C3.8

A   N
B   R
C   T
D   Z
E   Carbon nanotubes reinforce composite materials in sports equipment – It has a high tensile strength.

Carbon nanotubes in electronic devices – Its structure has delocalised electrons.

Various types of fullerenes to deliver drugs to treat cancer – Drug molecules can fit inside the cage structure.

Graphene to make flexible electronic displays – Its structure is flexible with delocalised electrons.

What you need to remember
fullerenes, hexagonal, reinforce, drugs, electronic, single

C3.9

A   outer electron of metal atom – pointing to a dot in one of the atoms in the diagram on the left
metal ion – pointing to one of the bigger circles in the diagram on the right
delocalised electrons – pointing to dots in the diagram on the right
metal atom – pointing to one of the biggest circles in the diagram on the left

B   a   metallic
b   shells
c   electrostatic
d   positively
e   crystals
f   three
g   delocalised

What you need to remember
giant, pattern, electrons, positively, electrostatic, electrons, metal

C3.10

A   (descriptions in *italic*, reasons in **bold**)
a   *Metals have high melting and boiling points* because **they have strong metallic bonding**.

b   *In pure metals the atoms are arranged in layers*. **This means they can be bent and shaped**.

c   **There are delocalised electrons in a sheet of metal**, so *metals are good conductors of electricity*.

d   *Metals are good conductors of thermal energy* because **their delocalised electrons can transfer this energy**.

e   *Pure gold is soft* because **its layers of atoms can slide over each other**.

B   Most alloys are a mixture of metals – *true*
Most alloys are softer than the pure metals used to make them – *false*
In an alloy, the different sized atoms make it easier for the layers in the giant structure to slide over each other – *false*
Alloys include delocalised electrons – *true*
Alloys are poor conductors of electricity – *false*

Corrected versions:
Most alloys are harder than the pure metals used to make them.
In an alloy, the different sized atoms make it more difficult for the layers in the giant structure to slide over each other.
Alloys are good conductors of electricity.

What you need to remember
metallic, melting, layers, soft, alloys, elements / metals, good, delocalised, heat / thermal

C3 Practice questions

01   covalent [1]
02.1 CH_4 [1]
02.2   one covalent bond [1]
02.3   Figure 1 shows the bonds but Figure 2 does not show the bonds; [1] Figure 1 suggests that the atoms are not touching each other in the molecule, when in fact they are [1]
03.1   Y [1]
03.2   W [1]
gold is a metal, so its boiling and melting points are high, and it conducts electricity [1]
03.3   Z [1]
03.4   element: carbon, as diamond [1]
compound: silicon dioxide [1]
03.5   soluble in water; [1] as substance is ionic [1]
04.1   the outer electron of a sodium atom is transferred to the outer shell of a chlorine atom; [1] this forms ions of formulae Na^+ and Cl^- [1]; the ions arrange themselves in a regular pattern; [1] there are strong electrostatic forces between the positive and negative ions [1]
04.2   there are strong electrostatic forces of attraction between the oppositely charged ions; [1] it takes a large amount of energy to disrupt these forces to melt the solid [1]
04.3   sodium chloride consists of positively and negatively charged ions; [1] the ions

are free to move when sodium chloride melts [1]

C4.1

A   relative atomic mass – A_r – the average mass of the atoms of an element compared with carbon-12

isotope – none – atoms of an element that have the same number of protons but a different number of neutrons

relative formula mass – M_r – the total of the relative atomic masses of each element in a substance, added up in the ratio shown in the chemical formula

B   75, 25, 35.5

C   a A_r of lithium $= \dfrac{(8 \times 6) + (92 \times 7)}{100} = 6.9$

b A_r of neon $= \dfrac{(91 \times 20) + (9 \times 22)}{100} = 20.2$

c A_r of bromine $= \dfrac{(51 \times 79) + (49 \times 81)}{100}$
$= 80.0$

D   a $35.5 \times 2 = 71$
b $12 + 16 = 28$
c $(2 \times 1) + 16 = 18$
d $12 + (2 \times 16) = 44$
e $(2 \times 27) + (3 \times 16) = 102$
f $63.5 + 32 + (3 \times 16) = 143.5$
g $1 + 14 + (3 \times 16) = 63$

What you need to remember
atomic, carbon, average / mean, atoms, total, formula

C4.2

A   concentration – the amount of solute dissolved in a given volume of solution

volume of solution – how much space a solution takes up

solvent – in a solution, the liquid that a substance is dissolved in

solute – in a solution, the substance that is dissolved in the solvent

solution – a mixture of substances, in which a solute is dissolved in a solvent

B   amount of solute – **g**
volume – dm³ or cm³
concentration – g/dm³ or g/cm³

C   amount of solute in g = **concentration in g/dm³ × volume of solution in dm³**

D   a   concentration (g/dm³) $= \dfrac{40\,g}{1\,dm^3}$
$= 40\,g/gm^3$

b   concentration (g/dm³) $= \dfrac{98\,g}{1000\,cm^3}$
$= \dfrac{90\,g}{1\,dm^3}$
$= 98\,g/gm^3$

c   concentration (g/dm³) $= \dfrac{4\,g}{250\,cm^3}$
$= \dfrac{4\,g}{0.25\,dm^3}$
$= 16\,g/gm^3$

E   a   amount of solute (g) $= 50\,g/dm^3 \times 1\,dm^3$
$= 50\,g$

b   amount of solute (g) $= 63\,g/dm^3 \times 0.5\,dm^3$
$= 31.5\,g$

What you need to remember
volume of solution in dm³, concentration in g/dm³

C4 Practice questions

01   3 [1]
02   5 [1]
03   45 g/dm³ [2]
04   3 g [2]
05.1   123.5 [2]
05.2   12.4 g [2]
05.3   two from: wear eye protection; tie back long hair; stand up; ensure that glass tube is removed from limewater before heating stops [2]
05.4   copper carbonate → **copper oxide** + **carbon dioxide** [1]
05.5   12.4 g [1]
05.6   one of the products is a gas; [1] the gas escapes so the mass of solid product is less than the mass of solid starting material [1]

C5.1

A   **ore** – a rock that contains a metal which can be extracted from the rock economically
oxidising – adding oxygen to a substance such as a metal
reducing – removing oxygen from a substance such as a metal oxide
reactivity series – a list of metals in order of their reactivity, with the most reactive at the top

B   LH column, from top: very slow reaction; reacts slowly with steam
RH column, from top: explode; fizz, giving off hydrogen and a salt; no reaction

C   a   magnesium + sulfuric acid →
magnesium sulfate + hydrogen
$Mg + H_2SO_4 \rightarrow MgSO_4 + H_2$

b   potassium + water →
potassium hydroxide + hydrogen
$2K + 2H_2O \rightarrow 2KOH + H_2$

What you need to remember
reactivity, most, vigorously, bottom, acids

C5.2

A   **W**
B   carbon and hydrogen
C   all boxes ticked
D   a   zinc
b   magnesium
c   tin
E   a   magnesium + zinc nitrate →
magnesium nitrate + zinc
b   lead + silver nitrate → lead nitrate + silver
c   magnesium + iron chloride →
magnesium chloride + iron
F   a $Mg(s) + ZnCl_2(aq) \rightarrow MgCl_2(aq) + Zn$

b $Cu(s) + 2AgNO_3(aq) \rightarrow$
$Cu(NO_3)_2(aq) + 2Ag(s)$

What you need to remember
more, less, solution, carbon, reactivity

C5.3

A   copper, gold
B   aluminium – *cannot*
calcium – *cannot*
copper – *can*
iron – *can*
lead – *can*
magnesium – *cannot*
sodium – *cannot*
tin – *can*

C   pencil circle – lead
blue circle – carbon
red circle – lead oxide
green circle – carbon dioxide

D   a   zinc oxide + carbon →
zinc + carbon dioxide
b   copper oxide + carbon →
copper + carbon dioxide
c   iron oxide + carbon →
iron + carbon dioxide

E   a $2PbO + C \rightarrow 2Pb + CO_2$
b $2ZnO + C \rightarrow 2Zn + CO_2$
c $2CuO + C \rightarrow 2Cu + CO_2$
d $2Fe_2O_3 + 3C \rightarrow 4Fe + 3CO_2$

What you need to remember
unreactive, below, carbon, oxygen, carbon dioxide, reduced, cannot

C5.4

A   Y
B   calcium – *reacts*
copper – *does not react*
gold – *does not react*
iron – *reacts*
lead – *reacts*
magnesium – *reacts*

C   potassium, sodium
D   hydrochloric – chlorides – chloride – Cl⁻
sulfuric – sulfates – sulfate – SO_4^{2-}
nitric – nitrates – nitrate – NO_3^-

E   a   chloride
b   sulfuric acid
c   iron, chloride

F   a   magnesium + sulfuric acid →
magnesium **sulfate** + hydrogen
b   zinc + **hydrochloric** acid →
zinc chloride + **hydrogen**
c   **iron** + sulfuric acid → i
ron **sulfate** + **hydrogen**

What you need to remember
acid, solution, evaporate, crystals

C5.5

A acid, insoluble, soluble, neutralisation, water, chloride, sulfate, nitrates

B hydrochloric acid, copper oxide, **copper chloride**, **water**

sulfuric acid, magnesium oxide, **magnesium sulfate**, **water**

nitric acid, **zinc oxide**, zinc nitrate, **water**

hydrochloric acid, magnesium oxide, magnesium chloride, **water**

sulfuric acid, copper oxide, copper sulfate, **water**

C a $MgSO_4$
   b $NaCl$
   c $NaNO_3$
   d $AlCl_3$
   e $ZnCl_2$
   f Na_2SO_4
   g $Cu(NO_3)_2$
   h $Al_2(SO_4)_3$
D **V, T, Y, U, X, Z, W**
E a $CuO + 2HCl \rightarrow CuCl_2 + H_2O$
   b $ZnO + 2HCl \rightarrow ZnCl_2 + H_2O$

What you need to remember

acid, products, sum, zero

C5.6

A acid and metal – salt and hydrogen
   acid and insoluble base – salt and water
   acid and alkali – salt and water
   acid and carbonate – salt, water, and carbon dioxide

B will not fizz when you add more: metal, carbonate
   use an indicator: alkali

C a $HCl(aq) + NaOH(aq) \rightarrow NaCl(aq) + H_2O(l)$
   b $H_2SO_4(aq) + CuCO_3(s) \rightarrow$
      $CuSO_4(aq) + H_2O(l) + CO_2(g)$
   c $2HCl(aq) + CaCO_3(s) \rightarrow$
      $CaCl_2(aq) + H_2O(l) + CO_2(g)$
   d $2HNO_3(aq) + CuCO_3(s) \rightarrow$
      $Cu(NO_3)_2(aq) + H_2O(l) + CO_2(g)$

What you need to remember

water, indicator, repeat, solution, salt, carbon dioxide

C5.7

A **acid** – This is a substance that produces hydrogen ions (H^+) in aqueous solution.
   alkali – This is a soluble hydroxide. It contains hydroxide ions (OH^-).
   base – This is any substance that can neutralise an acid.
   neutral – This is a substance that is neither acidic nor alkaline.
   pH scale – This tells you how acidic or alkaline a substance is.

B green – 7
   red – 0–6
   purple – 8–14

C When you add an alkali to an acid – the pH increases.

When you add an alkali to an acid – a neutralisation reaction occurs.
An alkaline solution – contains OH^- ions.
When you add an acid to an alkali – the pH decreases.
When you add an acid to an alkali – a neutralisation reaction occurs.
An acid – contains H^+ ions.

D an alkali is being added to an acid, since the pH is increasing

What you need to remember

Acids, alkali, hydroxide/OH^-, water, alkaline, less, more, neutral

C5 Practice questions

01.1 pour a sample of the solution into a test tube; [1] add a few drops of indicator solution; [1] compare the colour of the resulting solution to those on the indicator colour chart and estimate the pH [1]

01.2 **Z** [1]

01.3 **W** [1]

01.4 OH^- [1]

02.1 copper oxide [1]

02.2 2, 2 [2]

03.1 aq, l [2]

03.2 wearing eye protection, pour dilute sulfuric acid into a beaker and warm gently; [1] add zinc metal until no more reacts; [1] use a filter funnel and filter paper to filter into a beaker; [1] pour the filtrate into an evaporating basin; [1] use a Bunsen burner to heat the contents of the evaporating basin over a water bath; [1] when about half the water has evaporated, leave the remaining solution in a warm, dry place so that crystals form [1]

04.1 hydrochloric acid [1]

04.2 to remove unreacted zinc metal [1]

04.3 crystallisation [1]

C6.1

A electrolysis – using electricity to break down a substance
   electrolyte – a compound that is broken down by electricity
   anode – a positive electrode
   cathode – a negative electrode
   inert – describes a substance that is unreactive

B left, from top: anode, chlorine gas, liquid zinc chloride or electrolyte
   right, from top: cathode, zinc metal, liquid zinc chloride or electrolyte

C liquid, positively, cathode, negatively, anode, lose

What you need to remember

electricity, move, liquid, water, negative, cathode, positive, anode

C6.2

A a molecules
   b hydroxide
   c sodium
   d chloride
   e electrode
   f hydrogen
   g gas
   h negative
   i anode
   j hydrogen

B Positive copper ions (Cu^{2+}) are attracted to the cathode – *true*
   Copper metal is deposited at the anode – *false*
   Negative bromide ions (Br^-) are attracted to the anode – *true*
   Bromine forms at the cathode – *false*

   Corrected versions:
   Copper metal is deposited at the cathode.
   Bromine forms at the anode.

C copper chloride, silver nitrate

C6.3

A aluminium – electrolysis
   calcium – electrolysis
   iron – heating with carbon
   magnesium – electrolysis
   zinc – heating with carbon

B left, from top: **V, X**
   right, from top: **U, Y, W, Z**

D a aluminium oxide → aluminium + **oxygen**
      $2Al_2O_3(l) \rightarrow 4Al(l) + 3O_2(g)$
   b carbon + oxygen → **carbon dioxide**
      $C(s) + O_2(g) \rightarrow CO_2(g)$

What you need to remember

electrolysis, cryolite, aluminium, cathode, positive, carbon, dioxide, anodes

C6.4

A left: cathode (negative electrode)
   right: anode (positive electrode)
   bottom: electrolyte

B metal, cathode, non-metal, anode, negative, more, positive, oxygen

C lead bromide – molten, **lead**, bromine
   zinc chloride – molten, zinc, **chlorine**
   zinc chloride – solution, hydrogen, **chlorine**
   sodium chloride – solution, **hydrogen**, **chlorine**
   potassium bromide – solution, **hydrogen**, **bromine**
   copper sulfate – solution, **copper**, **oxygen**
   silver nitrate – solution, **silver**, **oxygen**

What you need to remember

hydrogen, oxygen, halogen

C6 Practice questions

01.1 unreactive [1]

01.2 anode: chlorine [1]
      cathode: zinc [1]

01.3 two from: carry out the demonstration in a fume cupboard; wear gloves; check if any students have asthma and send them out if necessary [2]

02.1 copper sulfate solution [1]

02.2 chlorine [1]

02.3 copper is deposited on it [1]

02.4 How does current affect the mass of copper deposited? [1]

02.5 points correctly plotted; [2] line of best fit passing through, or close to, all the points [1]

02.6 as current increases, the mass of copper deposited increases [1]

C7.1

A **exothermic reaction** – a reaction in which energy is transferred from the reacting substances to the surroundings – As the reaction happens, the temperature of the reaction mixture increases.

endothermic reaction – a reaction in which energy is transferred from the surroundings to the reacting substances – As the reaction happens, the temperature of the reaction mixture decreases.

B The products have a lower energy content than the reactants – *true*

The total energy content of the methane and oxygen is more than the total energy content of the carbon dioxide and water – *true*

During the reaction, the temperature of the surroundings decreases – *false*

Corrected version:
During the reaction, the temperature of the surroundings increases.

C sodium hydroxide solution and dilute nitric acid – 19, 45, **26** (red)

copper sulfate solution and magnesium powder – 21, **35**, 14 (red)

sulfuric acid and potassium hydroxide solution – 21, 51, **30** (red)

citric acid powder and sodium hydrogen carbonate powder – 22, 8, **–14** (blue)

What you need to remember

destroyed, from, to, endothermic

C7.2

A **Combustion** methane + oxygen →
carbon dioxide + water – *exothermic*

Thermal decomposition copper carbonate →
copper oxide + carbon dioxide – *endothermic*

B sports injury packs – endothermic – cools the surroundings hand warmers – exothermic – heats the surroundings

C green circle (advantages) – Barney
red circle (disadvantages – Catherine, Mary
black circle (neither advantages nor disadvantages) Sarah, Edward

What you need to remember

exothermic, endothermic

C7.3

A *y*-axis: energy
x-axis: progress of reaction
top box on graph: reactants
middle box on graph: energy change
bottom box on graph: products

B

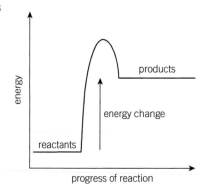

C Q

What you need to remember

collide, activation, profile, products

C7 Practice questions

01.1 to avoid energy transfer to the surroundings [1]

01.2 –6 [1]

01.3 ammonium chloride, ammonium nitrate [1]

01.4 copper sulfate (anhydrous), lithium chloride [1]

02.1 thermometer [1]

02.2 metal [1]

02.3 concentration of acid; [1] volume of acid; [1] amount of metal [1]

02.4 metal; [1] temperature of acid after reaction in °C [1]

03 the energy stored in the reactants is greater than the energy stored in the products; [1] this shows that energy is transferred to the surroundings / given out during the reaction [1]

C8.1

A time taken, mean rate of reaction

B measuring the decreasing mass of a reaction mixture – conical flask and top-pan balance – graph of mass of reacting mixture against time
measuring the volume of gas given off – conical flask and gas syringe – graph of volume of gas produced against time
measuring the decreasing amount of light passing through a reaction mixture – conical flask and X on piece of paper – graph of light transmitted against time

What you need to remember

reactant, product, graph, slope, steeper

C8.2

A a minimum
b energy

B increasing the energy that particles have when they collide – *reactions more likely*
decreasing the energy that particles have when they collide – *reactions less likely*
increasing the frequency of collisions between reacting particles – *reactions more likely*

C red circle: powder
green circle: powder

D powder: 0.04 g/s
big lumps: 2.0 g, 200 s, 0.01 g/s

What you need to remember

energy, minimum, activation, increases, collisions

8.3

A W, Z, Y, X, V

B more, more, higher, higher, greater

C temperature – independent variable
volume of acid – control variable
concentration of acid – control variable
length of magnesium ribbon – control variable
time for fizzing to stop – dependent variable

D a 10 °C
b 50 °C
c 5 s

What you need to remember

increases, increases, energy

C8.4

A The higher the concentration of reactants in solution – the shorter the time for the reaction to finish.
The higher the concentration of reactants in solution – the faster the rate.
The higher the concentration of reactants in solution – the greater the number of reactant particles moving around in a given volume.
The higher the concentration of reactants in solution – the more frequent the collisions.
The lower the concentration of reactants in solution – the less frequent the collisions.
The lower the concentration of reactants in solution – the slower the rate.
The lower the concentration of reactants in solution – the longer the time for the reaction to finish.
The lower the concentration of reactants in solution – the smaller the number of reactant particles moving around in a given volume.
The higher the pressure of reacting gases – the shorter the time for the reaction to finish.
The higher the pressure of reacting gases – the faster the rate.
The higher the pressure of reacting gases – the greater the number of reactant particles moving around in a given volume.
The higher the pressure of reacting gases – the more frequent the collisions.

B temperature, volumes, 2.0, fastest, increases, more, more

What you need to remember

collisions, increases, increases, increases

C8.5

A Catalysts increase the rate of chemical reactions – *true*

Catalysts are used up in reactions – *false*

A catalyst provides a different pathway for a reaction with a higher activation energy – *false*

A catalyst increases the frequency of collisions between reactant particles – *false*

When writing a chemical equation, you should not include the catalyst as one of the reactants – *true*

Corrected versions:

Catalysts are not used up in reactions.

A catalyst provides a different pathway for a reaction with a lower activation energy.

A catalyst increases the frequency of successful collisions between reactant particles.

B red arrow: vertical, with bottom of arrow on horizontal line labelled 'reactants' and top of arrow level with top of higher curve

blue arrow: vertical, with bottom of arrow on horizontal line labelled 'reactants' and top of arrow level with top of lower curve

C liver, liver, manganese(IV) oxide

What you need to remember

speeds, different, increase, temperature

C8.6

A A reversible reaction can go in two directions – *true*

In an equation for a reversible reaction, the substances on the left of the ⇌ symbol are called reactants – *true*

Indicators cannot undergo reversible reactions – *false*

Hydrated copper sulfate has no water of crystallisation – *false*

In a reversible reaction, the substances on the left of the ⇌ symbol are called the products – *false*

Hydrated copper sulfate forms anhydrous copper sulfate when water is added to it – *false*

In a reversible reaction, the reactants react together to form products – *true*

In a reversible reaction, the products react together to form reactants – *true*

Corrected versions:

Indicators can undergo reversible reactions.

Anhydrous copper sulfate has no water of crystallisation.

In a reversible reaction, the substances on the left of the ⇌ symbol are called the reactants.

Anhydrous copper sulfate forms hydrated copper sulfate when water is added to it.

B a   reversible
   b   ammonia
   c   reactant
   d   chloride
   e   ammonium
   f   eye

What you need to remember

products, reactants, reversible

C8.7

A **T**

B 860 kJ

C blue circle: hydrated copper(II) sulfate, $CuSO_4 \cdot 5H_2O$

pencil circle: anhydrous copper(II) sulfate, $CuSO_4$

red circle: anhydrous copper(II) sulfate, $CuSO_4$ and water, H_2O

green circle: ⇌

blue arrow: pointing from left to right

red arrow: pointing from right to left

What you need to know

endothermic, surroundings, equal, from, to

C8.8

A O

B U

C Z

D red line: top line
   blue line: lower line
   X: at the point where the two curved lines meet

What you need to remember

reactants, closed, equilibrium, forward, amounts

C8 Practice questions

01.1 The volume of gas increases quickly at first, and then more slowly. [1]

01.2 50 cm³/minute [2]

01.3 curved line levels off at 80 cm³; [1] slope of curve is steeper, so volume of 80 cm³ reached before 3 min [1]

02.1 $2HCl(\textbf{aq}) + CaCO_3(\textbf{s}) \rightarrow$
$\qquad CaCl_2(\textbf{aq}) + CO_2(\textbf{g}) + H_2O\ (\textbf{l})$ [2]

02.2 calcium chloride [1]

02.3 points correctly plotted [2]

02.4 smooth curve correctly drawn [1]

C9.1

A **mixture** – two or more substances that are mixed together but that are not joined together

hydrocarbon – a compound made up of hydrogen and carbon atoms only

fractions – hydrocarbons with similar boiling points that have been separated from crude oil

distillation – separating a liquid from a mixture by evaporation followed by condensation

alkanes – hydrocarbons with the general formula C_nH_{2n+2}. The first four are methane, ethane, propane, and butane

saturated hydrocarbon – a hydrocarbon that has single covalent bonds only between its carbon atoms

B finite, mud, many, hydrocarbons, alkanes

C methane – **CH₄**

ethane – C_2H_6,

propane – **C₃H₈**

butane – C_4H_{10},

D C_3H_8, C_5H_{12}, C_7H_{16}

What you need to remember

hydrocarbons, crude, hydrogen, only, single, general

C9.2

A C_5H_{12} – **lower**, less viscous, **higher**
   $C_{12}H_{26}$ – higher, **more viscous**, **lower**

B higher, less, more, fractional, molecules, processed

C gasoline / petrol – fuel for car engines

diesel oil / gas oil – fuel for diesel engines in cars, lorries and trains and fuel for boilers

kerosene – aircraft fuels

residue – making roads and flat roofs

refinery / liquefied petroleum gases (LPG) – fuel for heating, camping stoves and some vehicles

D left, from top: **2**, **8**, **4**, **1**
   right, from top: **3**, **5**, **6**, **7**

What you need to remember

fractions, distillation, size / length, more, molecules

C9.3

A The complete combustion of a hydrocarbon makes – carbon dioxide and water.

Burning methane in a gas cooker – transfers energy to the surroundings.

Burning diesel in a car – transfers energy to the surroundings.

A hydrocarbon is only useful as a fuel if – its flammability is high enough.

When a hydrocarbon burns – its carbon and hydrogen are oxidised.

B a $C_3H_8 + 5O_2 \rightarrow 3CO_2 + 4H_2O$
   b $CH_4 + 2O_2 \rightarrow CO_2 + 2H_2O$
   c $C_5H_{12} + 8O_2 \rightarrow 5CO_2 + 6H_2O$
   d $2C_2H_6 + 7O_2 \rightarrow 4CO_2 + 6H_2O$

What you need to remember

to, oxidised, water, fuels, combustion, monoxide

C9.4

A The products of cracking are less useful than the starting materials – *false*

The first step of cracking is to vaporise a heavy fraction from the distillation of crude oil – *true*

One method of cracking involves passing vapours from a heavy fraction of crude oil over a cold catalyst – *false*

One method of cracking involves mixing steam with vapour from a heavy fraction of crude oil and heating to a high temperature – *true*

Corrected versions:
The products of cracking are more useful than the starting materials.
One method of cracking involves passing vapours from a heavy fraction of crude oil over a hot catalyst.

B first test tube: orange
second test tube: colourless

C a red circles (alkenes): propene, ethane
blue circle (alkane): pentane

b red circle (alkene): propene
blue circle (alkane): hexane
$C_{12}H_{26} \rightarrow C_6H_{14} + 2C_3H_6$

What you need to remember
hydrocarbon, catalyst, steam, high, alkanes, polymers, bromine, colourless

C9 Practice questions

01 ethane [1]
02 propane [1]
03.1 11, 7, 8 [3]
03.2 heptane [1]
03.3 125 [2]
04.1 Hydrocarbons break down. [1]
04.2 it is a catalyst; [1] it speeds up the reaction without itself being used up [1]
04.3 pour a small amount of bromine water into a test tube; [1] bubble the substance into the bromine water; [1] if there is a colour change from orange to colourless, the substance is an alkene [1]

C10.1

A R
B U
C Z
D mixture, complex, compound, mixing
E petrol, deodorant, paint, hair shampoo, medicines, alloys, fertilisers, tinned soup, milk

What you need to remember
compounds, one, mixture, elements, boil, range, measured, properties

C10.2

A to show whether a something is a pure substance or a mixture – *correct use*
to separate substances – *correct use*
to measure boiling points – *incorrect use*
to identify substances – *correct use*
to measure melting points – *incorrect use*

B stationary – paper
mobile – solvent, for example water

C pen circle: around top blob
pencil circle: around bottom blob

D M, O, Q, N, R, L, P

What you need to remember
mixture, identify, R_f

C10.3

A hydrogen – a lighted splint pops
oxygen – a glowing splint relights
carbon dioxide – limewater turns milky (cloudy)
chlorine – damp litmus paper is bleached and turns white

B S
C W
D a gas: hydrogen
test: place a lighted splint in the gas
result: there will be a squeaky pop

b gas: carbon dioxide
test: bubble the gas through limewater
result: the limewater will go milky/cloudy

c gas: oxygen
test: place a glowing splint in the gas
result: the glowing splint will relight

What you need to know
lighted, pop, relights, oxygen, cloudy / milky, carbon dioxide, bleaches, white

C10 Practice questions

01 A glowing splint relights. [1]
02.1 a mixture that has been designed as a useful product [1]
02.2 iron fumarate [1]
02.3 5% [2]
02.4 226 [2]
03.1 step 1: so that the sample can move up the chromatography paper [1]
step 2: pencil marks do not dissolve in the chromatography solvent, but pen does [1]
step 3: to prevent the solvent evaporating into the room [1]
step 4: so that the R_f value can be calculated [1]
03.2 pigment: yellow [1]
reason: it has travelled furthest up the paper [1]
03.3 0.75 [3]
03.4 green pigment; [1] it has travelled further up the paper than the orange pigment [1]

C11.1

A P
B planet Earth formed – 4.6 billion years ago
intense volcanic activity – 4.6–3.6 billion years ago
algae first produced oxygen – 2.7 billion years ago
C second row, from left: carbon dioxide, water, methane, ammonia
third row, from left: oceans, photosynthesis
fourth row: oxygen

What you need to remember
volcanic, carbon dioxide, water, ammonia, plants, photosynthesis, increased

C11.2

A U, X, Y, V, Z, W, T
B animal, heated, coal, gas, trees, without, millions, plankton, mud, sediments, rock, natural gas
C nitrogen – 78%
oxygen – 21%
argon – 0.9%
carbon dioxide – 0.04%
other gases – trace amounts

What you need to remember
photosynthesis, sedimentary, fossil, nitrogen, oxygen, argon

C11.3

A water vapour, carbon dioxide, methane
B burning fossil fuels – *more carbon dioxide in the atmosphere*
adding waste to landfill sites – *more methane in the atmosphere*
farming cattle – *more methane in the atmosphere*
growing rice – *more methane in the atmosphere*
cutting down trees – *reduces the amount of carbon dioxide absorbed*
C next to Sun: **2**
next to Earth, from top: **4, 3, 1**
D Most scientists agree that a trend in global warming has started – *true*
Evidence in scientific journals does not support the existence of global warming – *false*
Evidence in scientific journals is peer reviewed (checked by other scientists) – *true*
Articles in the media about global warming are always true – *false*

Corrected versions:
Evidence in scientific journals supports the existence of global warming.
Articles in the media about global warming are not always true.

What you need to remember
high, increases, carbon dioxide, methane, journals, increase

C11.4

A Rising sea levels happen because of – ice caps melting.
Rising sea levels happen because of – water expanding at higher temperatures.
Climate change includes more frequent extreme weather events – such as more severe storms.
Changes in temperature and rainfall patterns – might result in certain crops growing better in some areas.
Changes in temperature and rainfall patterns – might result in certain crops growing less well in some areas.

Changes in temperature and rainfall patterns – might result in the extinctions of some species.

B carbon dioxide, greenhouse

C ways of reducing carbon dioxide: **1, 2, 4, 5**
ways of reducing methane: **3, 6**

What you need to remember
gases, temperatures, climate, reducing, fuels

C11.5

A sulfur dioxide – SO_2 – acid rain, breathing problems
nitrogen oxides – NO and NO_2 – acid rain, breathing problems
carbon monoxide – CO – toxic gas that can kill
soot (carbon particles, or particulates) – C – global dimming, damages lung cells and may cause cancer

B hydrogen, water, oxygen, dioxide, dioxide, oxygen, oxygen, nitrogen, not enough, monoxide, oxygen, monoxide, diesel, tiny, unburned.

What you need to remember
water, monoxide, carbon, dimming, sulfur dioxide, high, nitrogen, breathing, acid

C11 Practice questions

01 carbon monoxide – toxic to humans
particulates – global dimming
oxides of nitrogen – acid rain
carbon dioxide – climate change [3]

02.1 $N_2 + O_2 \rightarrow 2NO$ [3]

02.2 bars drawn to heights as follows:
London – 136, Manchester – 74, Portsmouth – 64, Scottish Borders – 27, South Wales – 70 [2 – 5 bars correct; 1 – 3 or 4 bars correct]

02.3 the value for Bristol is less than half the value for London; Bristol is a smaller city than London; there are fewer cars in Bristol [4]

02.4 $0.000136 \, g/m^3$ [2]

02.5 $53 \, \mu g/m^3$ [1]

02.6 one from: the calculated value is lower; there are fewer cars in Hull in the school holidays in August [1]

02.7 reasons: to improve health, to reduce acid rain
suggestions: reduce car use by improving public transport; reduce car use by encouraging walking and cycling; reduce car use by legislation/taxes [6]

C12.1

A crude oil – finite
crops used to make biofuels – renewable
coal – finite
softwoods – renewable

B wood – **window frames** – PVC
sisal – **ropes** – poly(propene)
cotton – covering food – **cling film**
wool – **clothes** – **acrylic**

C a over time, from 1950 to 2010, the estimated reserves of copper have increased
b technological advances mean that it is now possible/economically feasible to extract copper from sources that copper could not be extracted from in the past
c new reserves may be discovered at any time

What you need to remember
resources, renewable, natural, unknowns

C12.2

A safe, is not, low, low, rainwater

B from top: dissolved, sand, solid, sterilised, chlorine, ultraviolet

C In countries with wet climates and plenty of natural sources of fresh water, potable water can be obtained from seawater – *false*
Most potable water that is obtained from seawater is obtained by distillation – *true*
Distillation is one method of desalination – *true*
The energy costs of the distillation of seawater are low – *false*
A process called reverse osmosis uses membranes to remove dissolved salts from water – *true*
Reverse osmosis involves heating, so it requires more energy than distillation – *false*

Corrected versions:
In countries with wet climates and plenty of natural sources of fresh water, potable water is not obtained from seawater.
The energy costs of the distillation of seawater are high.
Reverse osmosis does not involve heating, so it requires less energy than distillation.

What you need to remember
source, sterilising, ultraviolet, dry, distillation and reverse, high

C12.3

A first row: Screening removes big, solid objects and then grit.
third row: Air bubbles through the effluent. Aerobic bacteria break down harmful microorganisms and organic matter.
fourth row, from left: The effluent flows into a river; The sludge can be used as a source of renewable energy.

What you need to remember
big, sedimentation, sludge, aerobic, anaerobic, water

C12.5

A environment, raw materials, packaging, reusing, disposing, water, sources, wastes

B inputs: raw materials, energy, water
outputs: waste that goes into rivers and the sea, solid waste, emissions to the atmosphere, other products made alongside the product

C can be given a numerical value: raw materials needed, water required in manufacture, fuel used in distribution, waste gases
cannot easily be given a numerical value: impact of noise during manufacture, impact on pedestrians of distribution vehicles, impact of waste gases on human health, impact on wildlife of waste that enters rivers

What you need to remember
environmental, products, life cycle, raw, using, possible, opinion

C12.6

A a materials
b quarrying
c reuse
d recycling
e recycled

B Crushing glass bottles, melting them, and making new bottles – *recycling*
Giving your coat to your little sister or brother when it is too small for you – *reuse*
Collecting gold from used mobile phones, melting the gold, and making rings from it – *recycling*
Giving your old mobile phone to a charity that makes sure it works before giving it to someone who cannot afford to buy their own – *reuse*

C from start: separated, shredded, melted, cooled, new

What you need to remember
metal, environmental, money, fuels, reduces

C12 Practice questions

01.1 extracting oil from oil wells under the sea to make plastic – obtaining and processing raw materials

messaging friends – using the product

giving the phone to a younger brother or sister when it is no longer fashionable – using the product

extracting metals from their ores to make circuit components – obtaining and processing raw materials

putting together the components in a plastic or metal case – making the product and packaging

recycling phone components – disposing of the product and packaging [4 – all

correct; 3 – 4 or 5 correct; 2 – 2 or 3
correct; 1 – 1 correct]

01.2   Action 1
stage: using the product [1]
how environmental impact is reduced:
reduce pollution resulting from
electricity generation [1]

Action 2
stage: making the product and
packaging [1]
how environmental impact is reduced:
reduce use of raw materials and
waste associated with obtaining and
processing them [1]

Action 3
stage: disposing of the product and
packaging [1]
how environmental impact is reduced:
reduce amount of waste that must be
disposed of [1]

02.1   sulfate [1]

02.2   30.5 mg [2]

02.3   43 litres [3]

02.4   it is not possible to drink 43 litres of
water in one day [1]

Appendix 1: the periodic table

key

relative atomic mass
atomic symbol
name
atomic (proton) number

Example: 1 **H** hydrogen 1

1	2											3	4	5	6	7	0
																	4 **He** helium 2
7 **Li** lithium 3	9 **Be** beryllium 4											11 **B** boron 5	12 **C** carbon 6	14 **N** nitrogen 7	16 **O** oxygen 8	19 **F** fluorine 9	20 **Ne** neon 10
23 **Na** sodium 11	24 **Mg** magnesium 12											27 **Al** aluminium 13	28 **Si** silicon 14	31 **P** phosphorus 15	32 **S** sulfur 16	35.5 **Cl** chlorine 17	40 **Ar** argon 18
39 **K** potassium 19	40 **Ca** calcium 20	45 **Sc** scandium 21	48 **Ti** titanium 22	51 **V** vanadium 23	52 **Cr** chromium 24	55 **Mn** manganese 25	56 **Fe** iron 26	59 **Co** cobalt 27	59 **Ni** nickel 28	63.5 **Cu** copper 29	65 **Zn** zinc 30	70 **Ga** gallium 31	73 **Ge** germanium 32	75 **As** arsenic 33	79 **Se** selenium 34	80 **Br** bromine 35	84 **Kr** krypton 36
85 **Rb** rubidium 37	88 **Sr** strontium 38	89 **Y** yttrium 39	91 **Zr** zirconium 40	93 **Nb** niobium 41	96 **Mo** molybdenum 42	[98] **Tc** technetium 43	101 **Ru** ruthenium 44	103 **Rh** rhodium 45	106 **Pd** palladium 46	108 **Ag** silver 47	112 **Cd** cadmium 48	115 **In** indium 49	119 **Sn** tin 50	122 **Sb** antimony 51	128 **Te** tellurium 52	127 **I** iodine 53	131 **Xe** xenon 54
133 **Cs** caesium 55	137 **Ba** barium 56	139 **La*** lanthanum 57	178 **Hf** hafnium 72	181 **Ta** tantalum 73	184 **W** tungsten 74	186 **Re** rhenium 75	190 **Os** osmium 76	192 **Ir** iridium 77	195 **Pt** platinum 78	197 **Au** gold 79	201 **Hg** mercury 80	204 **Tl** thallium 81	207 **Pb** lead 82	209 **Bi** bismuth 83	[209] **Po** polonium 84	[210] **At** astatine 85	[222] **Rn** radon 86
[223] **Fr** francium 87	[226] **Ra** radium 88	[227] **Ac*** actinium 89	[261] **Rf** rutherfordium 104	[262] **Db** dubnium 105	[266] **Sg** seaborgium 106	[264] **Bh** bohrium 107	[277] **Hs** hassium 108	[268] **Mt** meitnerium 109	[271] **Ds** darmstadtium 110	[272] **Rg** roentgenium 111	[285] **Cn** copernicium 112	[286] **Nh** nihonium 113	[289] **Fl** flerovium 114	[289] **Mc** moscovium 115	[293] **Lv** livermorium 116	[294] **Ts** tennessine 117	[294] **Og** oganesson 118

*The lanthanides (atomic numbers 58–71) and the actinides (atomic numbers 90–103) have been omitted.

Relative atomic masses for **Cu** and **Cl** have not been rounded to the nearest whole number.